Morganton 31

Andrew Baird
1 3/4 yds Cambrick — "/0

Joshua Connelly Dr
1 yd Cambrick 81/4 Ct

David Tate Dr
1 set of tea cups and saucers  75    75

Isaac Ferrell Dr
1 1/4 of homspun — 50   50

Perry G. Reynolds Dr
2 yards black cambrick at 50 — 1
1 yard of cambrick 62 1/2 1 yd leno muslin 1
1 lb of powder 50 1 Penknife 43 3/4          93 3/4
1/2 yard of wire 18 3/4 2 yds ribbon at 18 3/4   56 1/4

Alexander Erwin Dr
3 lb of coffee — 1/   1

Maj. John McGimsey Dr
1/2 doz Plates — 75
1/2 do Cups & Saucers — 75
1/2 do Saucers — 25

William W Erwin Dr
1 lb Wood screw — 18 3/4

"Hand-written pages are reproduced from a Morganton general store ledger, 1816-1817."

*To Darcy –*
*For all you've done –*
*Erwin 2020*

# The Village That Disappeared

# The Village That Disappeared

Susan Graham Erwin

LANEY-SMITH, INC.
Charlotte, NC

Published by Laney-Smith, Inc.
1370 Briar Creek Road
Charlotte, North Carolina 28205

© 1996 by Susan Graham Erwin. All rights reserved. No part of this book may be reproduced or transmitted in any form or by any means, electronic or mechanical, including photocopying, recording, or by any information storage and retrieval system, without permission in writing from the owner of the copyright.

Published 1996

Printed in the United States of America
by
Delmar Printing Company, Charlotte, NC

Library of Congress Catalog Number 95-81871

ISBN 0-9624488-6-9

### In Appreciation

I wish to express my appreciation to Claudia Erwin Powe Watkins for her continued interest in this book and for the many letters she wrote to relatives to announce its printing; to Claudia Erwin Watkins Belk for her interest and suggestions as to its printing and binding; to Roger Gant for his encouragement to me to continue to its completion; and to Mark Erwin, who had the original manuscript copied in his office.

Susan Graham Erwin

*Tales of Long-Ago
Morganton, North Carolina
and its Environs —
A Southern Town that is
different from every other
Town in the State
and probably different from every
Town in every other State.*

## THE VILLAGE THAT DISAPPEARED

### To The Reader

This book is not a history.

It is a collection of true stories about the once little village of Morganton, North Carolina that, due to unprecedented and astonishing events in its past, was referred to in early days as "The Gem in the Wilderness."

These unusual events caused it to become different from every other town in the state, and probably different from every town in every other state—a fact that many persons appear to have forgotten.

It was named Morganton in honor of General Daniel Morgan, a hero of the Revolutionary War, and is situated in the piedmont area of North Carolina within view of the Blue Ridge Mountains, which is one of the most beautiful regions of the state.

Since the book is not a history, I have not burdened it with dates and references, which can be found in printed records concerning whatever events of importance I have included. My purpose, rather, is to tell of events as they occurred in a continuing story-type fashion, and to include a little about the personalities of the people involved.

The sketches were written at the request of a number of young relatives, who insist that these interesting and unique stories of long ago should not be forgotten and lost in the crowding mists of time, but should be recorded for people to read and enjoy in years to come.

*Part One* (1752-1900) deals with the origin and early days of the village, its people and those of its environs. Its stories tell of pioneer days, the Revolutionary War, the times prior to and during the Civil War, the period of Reconstruction that followed the Civil War, and ends with the turn of the century.

In this section the Erwin family, one of the first to pioneer into the area, is dealt with more fully than any other, simply because I have been able to learn more about it. However, it possesses definite historic value in that it can be said to be a prototype of other families that came into the area at about the same time and lived under similar conditions during the years that followed.

*Part Two* (1900-1920) begins with the turn of the century and deals with the little town of Morganton, its people and those of its environs as I knew them in my childhood and youth.

I was born there in 1909 and lived there until I was grown, and as I look back across the eighty-seven years that have passed since that time, it seems hardly possible that the village as I knew it could have actually ever existed, so changed has it become today.

Still, the more I think about it, the more vividly certain persons and scenes appear before me. Even brief conversations come back so clearly that I can repeat them almost verbatim, while with many longer conversations I am still aware of the intent of the speakers. Nor did I forget the many elderly persons living amongst us at that time, who exerted a definite and lasting impression upon us — the so-called "ladies and gentlemen of the Old School" — whose like we do not see today.

They had gone through the heartbreak of the Civil War and the devastation and poverty of the Reconstruction Period that followed the war, but they still held fast to the customs, manners, and morals of a more gracious day that had long since vanished and could never come again.

It is only natural that with tales passed down through the years some should vary in details from others, but I have done my best to tell them just as they were told to me.

Susan Graham Erwin

## PART ONE
## (1752-1900)

1. The First Description of the Morganton Area (1752)—The First Description of the Village of Morganton, its People, and those of its Environs (1816-1818)—Two Hangings in the Village  1

2. The Two Brothers—Indian War Paint on the Big Oak Tree—Forts of Refuge—The Battle of Kings Mountain —"Alexander Erwin, Lord of the Mountains"  11

3. A Tragic Death—The Log Courthouse with a Whipping Post and Stocks—Pretty Polly's Son  19

4. The Halcyon Years—The Discovery of Gold (1839-1840)—The Supreme Court of North Carolina—Why Morganton was Called "The Gem in the Wilderness"  26

5. The Civil War (1861-1865)—Bloody Kirk and The Mountain Desperadoes—The Home Guards—The "Lion Hearted Host"  39

6. A Dangerous Stagecoach Ride—When the Yankee Cavalry Came to Morganton—The Surrender, Heartbreak and Tragedy—The End of an Era  51

## PART TWO
## (1900-1920)

1. "Ladies and Gentleman of the Old School"—Horses and Mules—Surreys, Carryalls and Buggies—Covered Wagons and Mountainfolk—Bucephalus—Miss Sue—Polly Malindy—Old Man Ballew—Confederate Memorial Day—Beautiful Aunt Claudia—The Witch Lady—The Wooden Leg ... 63

2. Gasoline Machines—The Stagecoach—The Train—Miss Maggie Jenks—The Sea Captain and His Lady—Mary Louise and Elizabeth Matilda—Two Tragic Romances—Edward ... 79

3. A Visit to a Different World—Hat Tubs—Feather Beds—Chemises—The Chicken Thief—The Ten Commandments—The Crazy Woman—When the Kitchen Caught Fire—The Chemise That Could Fly—The High Buggy and the Low Buggy—Good Manners ... 98

4. Two Ladies Marooned in a Flood—Civil War Tales—The Wedding Dress in the Parlor Chimney—The Christmas Log—Starvation Parties ... 112

5. The Wedding Reception of Governor Zebulon Vance—Lady La Paloma—The Fire Horses—The Angora Goat—Two Different Trips to Town—Edward ... 124

6. Family House Parties—The Rites of Venus—"The Prime Totin' Man"—The Cave—"Going Adventuring"—Sarah's House—The Story Telling Hill—Flying Squirrels ... 137

7. A Heart-Breaking Scheme—Going to Willow Tree Colored Baptist Church with Estelle—Edward—A Shocking Plan ... 150

8. Bessie Cow—Pete and Repeat—Village Scandals—The Fancy Lady—Aunt Matilda's Portrait—Edward ... 157

9. The Last House Party—A Lesson in Love and Generosity—The Angel of Death ... 170

10. Voices in the Wind ... 177

# PART ONE
(1752-1900)

PART ONE
(1752-1900)
*The First Description of the Morganton Area (1752)*
*The First Description of the Village, its People and Those
of its Environs (1816-1818)*
*Two Hangings in the Village*

1.

Tradition tells us that at first there was only a spring of fresh, clear water that gushed from the side of the hill close to the present- day Grace Episcopal Church and only a few blocks from where the Courthouse stands in the center of town. We are also told that as time went by the spring gained a name.

Certain records state that it was called Alder Springs because of the alder trees that stood nearby, and that this was the first name of the little village of Morganton that would eventually be established there. There is also a tradition that says it was called Laurel Springs (sometimes spelled Lorrel) and was probably named for the thick leaved laurel bushes with their pink and white blossoms that clustered about it.

All around it, so far as the eye could see, even as far away as the Blue Ridge Mountains that towered in the west, was only a wilderness threaded here and there by winding buffalo trails and Indian trading paths. However, there must have been times when pioneers, pressing ever westward, camped beside the spring or paused for a drink of cold, clean water. One of them may even have been Daniel Boone, for it is known that he passed that way.

We have learned that the first man to write about this vast unknown wilderness in the piedmont section of North Carolina was Gottlieb Spangenburg, a Bishop of the Moravian Church, who, with his little band of followers, came riding into the area in 1752 searching unsuccessfully for a place to build a Moravian settlement.

He was probably following a buffalo trail or an Indian trading path that ran through the dense forests and lush, grassy meadows, since there were no known ways to guide him; and in his diary he wrote, "We are here in a region that has seldom been trod by the foot of man since the creation of the world."

He and his little group of brethren chose a camping place in a green low-lying meadow on the westward side of the Catawba River. From there they made several hazardous expeditions into the surrounding territory but never found what they sought. According to tradition, the few settlers in the area thought the Moravians were Quakers and, because of this, the place where they camped is still called Quaker Meadows, "the meadows where the Quakers camped."

While the first description of which we know about the Morganton area was written by Bishop Spangenburg in 1752, the next we have found was penned in the journal of a young stranger named Silas McDowell in 1816 and 1818.

By that time, the village of Morganton was already in existence. It had been established as the county seat in the newly formed county of Burke (1777), which was named in honor of a governor of the state and Silas McDowell described it as it was the first time he set eyes upon it.

He had just arrived in Morganton after a long and tiring journey from Charleston, South Carolina in a wagon drawn by six stalwart mules. The cross-country wagons of that time took thirty-six days to make the trip, given fair weather. If oxen were used instead of mules, as was sometimes the case, it took even longer.

The route they followed was originally an old Indian trading path that began over the mountains in Tennessee, ran down through the valley of the Catawba River and passed through or near the village of Morganton. Turning southward, it crossed South Carolina, bearing eastward and ending at Charleston by the sea, which, according to tradition, was a popular gathering place for certain Indian tribes that assembled nearby at specified times for trading or to hold pow-wows that included conferences, feasting, and dancing.

The young Silas McDowell was a tailor by trade. He planned to settle in Morganton and to make his living there. He records in his journal that the first person he met after his arrival in the village was Colonel Thomas Walton, a gentleman who kept a store in the center of town facing the public square. Colonel Walton greeted him graciously and took him across the street to a small brick inn operated by a kind, friendly, well-educated old lady.

After Silas had made an inspection of the public square and the buildings that faced it, the lady innkeeper inquired how he liked the place, and he replied that the village of Morganton "as the county seat of the wealthy county of Burke, was a decidedly shabby place"—implying that the wealth of the area was obviously in the hands of the planters in the surrounding valley rather than in those of the villagers.

# Chapter One

The Courthouse, he wrote, was "a plain frame weather-beaten structure and there was a jail of hewn logs with one door and two windows secured with iron bars, while nearby stood a whipping post and stocks." The only building facing the Courthouse that was neat and clean looking, he recorded, was the white painted home of John Caldwell that stood on the north, and "all other buildings on that side were of logs except for a frame building in which Colonel W. Erwin kept a bank and his sons and James Avery a store."

On the south was a large unpainted frame house where lived an old German man and his wife, and not far from the inn was the dwelling of David Tate, "an unpainted rambling frame building, long and lonesome looking and suggestive of rats." Behind these buildings and a little farther back were several other structures, "a few of which had some claim to architectural taste, and this was all that made up the village."

The young tailor was enchanted, however, by the little town "as a standpoint to look over the most magnificent valley in the world. This beautiful valley," he wrote, "seems as if it is a lovely scroll unrolled to the eyes of the spectator, encircled by a bold framework of blue mountains faraway to the west and northwest and they appear to give the horizon an upward tilt and present many bold and a few fantastic points."

When he asked his landlady at the inn about a church, she replied there was none. About twenty years before, she told him, a bright young Presbyterian minister named John McCamey Wilson organized a church in a beautiful stretch of valley that was called Quaker Meadows just across the river, not far from town.

He stayed twenty years and married Mary, one of the daughters of Colonel Alexander Erwin—"a spritely young woman generally called Pretty Polly"—but the children came so fast that his salary was insufficient to support them. Because of this, he was forced to leave, but he came back once a year to administer the sacrament to the old members of his flock.

When the lady innkeeper learned that the young tailor planned to live in Morganton, she said that, since this would bring him into contact with the citizens of Burke County, he should know something about them; so she would "exhibit for him a kind of portrait gallery of the families that occupy the front rank of Burke's social circle."

"I will begin," she told him, "with the old patriarchs of the county—the few survivors from whom have descended the very best families in the county. The oldest man among them is Arthur Erwin on Upper Creek; he was once a man of sound, practical common sense; a plain, unassuming man. He is high up in eighty and is the father of Colonel William W. Erwin of Belvedere.

"The next is Colonel Alexander Erwin, brother of Arthur and twelve years younger; their lands join; they are quite unalike in character, Alexander having been devoted to books and the current literature of the age, and withal, when young a wit and a dandy; his best representative is his son Colonel James Erwin, Clerk of the County Court.

"The next is Colonel Waighstill Avery of Swan Ponds. He was once a great lawyer and an amiable man but is confined at home with weakness in his limbs; and he is represented by his only son named Isaac, lately married to Harriet, eldest daughter of Colonel William W. Erwin of Belvedere."

After these, the lady named in order other men: "John Rutherford of Muddy Creek, who is represented by his only surviving son, John. The next is Colonel John Carson of Buck Creek, whose last wife was the widow of Gentleman Joseph McDowell; and John Murphy, who is a great financier and has only one son, Jack."

Then she named "Colonel John McGimpsey of Linville Valley, who has two sons, John and William—clever young men; old David Forney of Upper Creek, very clever but made a fool of himself by marrying a young girl when he was over sixty—he will be represented by a large family of children. Besides these, there is old Colonel Baird of Gunpowder Creek and old Sam Newton who married a Tate; three Perkins brothers on John's River, but Jo has the prettiest daughters. " She also named Major Hiland, who married a Perkins; Dr. Bouchell and a few men who lived at some distance from Morganton; and "old David Tate, who lives in the village."

"Dave," she added, "is a kind-hearted wicked man in whom good and evil are about equally mixed. He is very popular with the poor and represents Burke County in the legislature."

She also named five brothers who owned much property and were considered to be rich, but "are not tolerated by good society, although some of them had married good, kind and pious wives. The real drawbacks of the family are Ephraim, Sam, James and Bill."

She said, "Jim and Bill are idiots, nearly, and Sam keeps a black woman for a wife, and that woman is the greatest curiosity I ever beheld. She is coal black, but has form and features that would be a good model for a statuary chiseling out of a Hermes. There is another batch of brothers that may be called the Arabs of our respectable society but have no part of it."

She gave the full names of all of these unworthy citizens, but it is perhaps best to leave them unnamed and to turn to younger men whom she added next in line. She spoke of Charles McDowell of Quaker Meadows, and also, of Abe Fleming of Fleming's Island as being "amiable men." In fact, she said, there were "scores of amiable young men in the area."

On learning that Silas McDowell was a tailor, the kind old lady said she felt it was her duty to warn him that Burke society would not appreciate him at his true value because he was a "mechanic" and he would be watched closely, particularly by "the parents of silly young girls." They had reasons for this, she added, and then she told him of a young man from Massachusetts, hired as a tanner on Colonel Avery's plantation, who eloped with the Colonel's daughter.

"He turned out to be one of the most fiendish villains Burke County was ever cursed with," she said, "and the first time Colonel Avery met him after this he tried to cane him. Instead, the Colonel got soundly drubbed himself, but he obtained a divorce for his daughter."

There were several other "mechanics" who had invaded the area, she continued, "who had married daughters of prominent men, then turned out to be incorrigible rascals, so the girls' fathers had to get divorces for them, also." Consequently, she advised the young tailor to "go slow" for a while until he had developed a positive character.

Silas McDowell continued to write in his journal and in 1817, the year after his arrival, he recorded that conditions had begun to change in the village. "A Presbyterian church was built, Mr. Chancery Edy being the preacher, and Mr. Thomas Walton an elder. Male and female academies were constructed. Mr. Walton built a brick house northwest of the Courthouse and a brick jail was also built. Colonel Avery put an addition on his residence at Swan Ponds Plantation and Colonel James Erwin built a brick mansion above the juncture of Upper Creek and the Catawba River."

The kind and pious old lady who kept the inn and the young tailor soon became good friends and she told him she had decided to tell him "the inmost secret of my life," which she had never told to anyone. Instead, she had "kept it pent up in my breast for more than forty years."

She stated that she had come originally from Ireland and her parents died before she was five years old, leaving her an heiress with two thousand pounds. She was well educated and, being considered to be a beauty, she had many suitors.

She fell in love with and became betrothed to a young man who, she confessed, looked very much like the young tailor. They planned to marry and elope to America, but her uncle, who was her guardian, opposed the match because the young man was poor and had "no landed property." Instead, the uncle insisted that she marry a friend of his, a man of property who was thirty years older than she.

When she refused to do this, the uncle locked her in her room and later took her on board a ship bound for Charleston, South Carolina. The next day he and his family came to the ship to take leave of her and with them was his rich older friend and a Catholic priest. Her uncle stated that the priest was there to marry her and his friend, but she still refused to obey him.

"Of what happened next I have no recollection," the lady said, for she fell ill and was too weak and dazed to think. When her mind returned, she was in the city of Charleston, South Carolina in a boarding house, "utterly devoid of strength, recovering from a severe attack of typhoid fever," and attended by a doctor and her new elderly husband. Through the following years the husband proved to be a kind and honorable man. He made her a good husband, so she did her best to make him a good wife.

By the time she met the young tailor, her husband had become too old to run the inn, so she ran it herself. However, she never ceased to grieve over her sad story or to miss her young sweetheart in Ireland, whom she never saw again.

For many years her husband was sheriff and kept the jail and during that time an event took place that made her realize that there were other persons who experienced grief that was as deep as her own, which helped her to go on with her life in the village.

This event occurred when a handsome young man, eighteen years of age, was brought to the jail for horse stealing. This was a grievous crime in that day because to take away a man's horse was to deprive him of his main means of transportation and prevent his performing many duties needed to support himself. The young man's name was John Handrakes and he was the only child of a poor widow, a "fine and noble woman" who lived in the mountains a good distance from the village.

One day the boy set out on the only horse his mother possessed to visit his uncle, who lived in another part of the mountains. On his way home the horse died, so he had to continue his long journey on foot, and along the way he was overtaken by a gentlemanly looking stranger on a fine horse, who remarked that the young man looked tired.

He said he had become weary of riding and offered to let the young man ride his horse to the forks of the road, which was some distance farther on, while he took a short cut through the woods on foot—after which he would join him at the forks and take back his horse. The young man, thankful for a ride, accepted his offer, but when he reached the designated place he was met by a group of men who arrested him and took him to Morganton to be tried for horse stealing.

In the village he was tried and sentenced to hang for stealing the horse, although he never ceased insisting that he was innocent and told them that if they killed him his mother would most certainly die from the shock and grief of his death.

His mother came to his hanging in Morganton and stoically watched his death pangs, showing no emotion when he was hanged; and this caused many persons to think her an uncaring and hard-hearted mother, which was not the case. When they placed him in his coffin she leaned lovingly over him, did her best to compose his distorted features, smoothed his hair, embraced him tenderly and kissed him on the forehead.

Because evening was coming on, several persons, pitying her, urged her to delay her journey back to the mountains and to stay overnight with them, but this she refused to do.

"I know you mean well, but it will do no good. My heart is broken," she said, and gathering her mantle about her, she hurried through the crowd and started on her long walk home.

The next day about two miles west of Morganton, some passersby saw a woman lying asleep beside the road, but, on going closer, they found it was the broken-hearted mother and she was not asleep but dead. Not knowing where she lived or who her people were, or if she had any, they wrapped her in her mantle and buried her beside the road where she had fallen and died, thinking someone would surely claim the body and give it decent burial.

"No one did," the landlady said, "so the poor woman still lies beneath the weeds and briers beside the road in her lonely grave. Many years later a notorious thief was hanged in another state and before he died he confessed that he was the man on the stolen horse who had caused the death of the innocent young man."

John Handrakes was not the only person to be hanged in Morganton in the early days, however. A number of years after Handrakes died, a pretty young mountain wife was hanged there for killing her husband, Charlie Silver, with an ax. Her name was Frankie (Frances) Stuart Silver and she lived in an isolated spot in the mountains near the foot of Mount Mitchell. Many conflicting stories have been told about this tragedy and no crime in the region has shocked the people so greatly, which is confirmed by the tales about Frankie that have lived on through the years in song and story.

The known facts are that Charlie Silver, an attractive and popular young man, left Frankie and their infant daughter in their cabin several days before the Christmas of 1831, saying he was "going down to the Gap to get his Christmas whiskey," although there was bad weather and snow was on the ground; so Frankie suspected that he was going to see another woman, of whom she was jealous.

After Christmas when several men went to the Silvers' cabin to get him to go hunting, he was not there. Frankie told them he had not come home. They feared he had run into trouble of some sort or, since the river had frozen over, he had fallen through the ice and drowned, but he was not found.

A hunting dog began to sniff about the place and the body was discovered. It had been hacked to pieces and some parts were found under the cabin floor and some in a hole not far from the cabin where hogs were killed. In that spot was also found a metal piece from one of Charlie's hunting boots.

It was discovered that he had come home before Christmas, as he had promised and that he and Frankie had a quarrel and they immediately surmised that she had killed him.

She was accused of murder and brought to the jail in Morganton. Aided by men in her family, she escaped in a load of hay, wearing men's clothing, but she was caught and brought back to the jail. There are stories that say she escaped a second time, fled to nearby Rutherfordton County and lived there for some time with her hair cut short and wearing men's clothing. She was caught again, brought back to Morganton and tried at the courthouse. She was convicted of the crime and hanged on a large oak tree on July 12, 1883, on what was then called Damon's Hill. It was not far from the courthouse, and later became the John Dickson property next to the site of Broad Oaks Sanatorium on what is now Valdese Avenue.

# Chapter One

In that day the law did not permit a person charged with a crime to testify on his or her own behalf, because it was thought the truth would not be told. However, many years after her death, when he was an old man, Nicholas Woodfin, who was her lawyer and well-known throughout the state, told President Battle of the University at Chapel Hill, who published the facts in a book he wrote, that Frankie did not kill Charlie willfully but in self defense and that, if she had been permitted to tell her story to the jury, as she had told it to him, she would not have been hanged.

During her quarrel with Charlie, he began to beat her with a stick, the lawyer said, and in terror, she grabbed up an ax and struck him in the neck in an effort to save her life. "Her death was a miscarriage of justice," he told Dr. Battle. "She was unjustly hanged, and, ironically, the law that caused her death was changed not long after she died."

The family of Charlie Silver was large and well-known throughout the mountain area, as was the family of Frankie (the Stuarts), and on the day of the hanging a large crowd gathered in Morganton. As she stood on the scaffold just before she was hanged, the attending preacher asked if she had anything to say in the last moments of her life on earth.

She took a step forward and appeared to be about to speak, but her father called out from the crowd, "Don't talk! Die with it in you, Frankie!" She obeyed him and remained silent.

This caused many persons to think her father and perhaps some of the men in her family had a part in the murder of Charlie. Added to this was the fact that Frankie was a small, slim young woman who was not likely to be strong enough to hack apart a tall man's body with an ax, lift the puncheon floor of the cabin, dig a grave beneath it and bury parts of the body there and parts in the pit where hogs were slaughtered not far from the cabin, which had been done.

On the day of the hanging my grandfather, Colonel Joseph J. Erwin of Bellevue, then a boy of about fourteen years of age, rode into Morganton on horseback and joined the crowd. He heard the preacher's question to Frankie, noted that she appeared about to speak and then fell silent after being ordered to do so by her father. Unable to bear seeing her hanged, my grandfather mounted his horse and rode away, but he repeated to his family what Frankie's father had said to her—which are the same words I have read in printed accounts written by different persons.

It was the custom in that day for the bodies of persons who had been hanged to be given to medical students for dissection, but Frankie's family wanted to take her home for burial, so they left Morganton as quickly as possible. The weather was hot and the body was decomposing rapidly, so they stopped overnight at the Bruckhorn Tavern on the Yellow Mountain Road. They buried her there and today her grave can be found in that wild and inaccessible spot near the old tavern about eight miles from Morganton.

As the years went by and after the young tailor, Silas McDowell, the lady innkeeper, John Handrakes, and Frankie Silver had passed away, other, less gruesome tragedies were to take place in the little town, but it was also to experience astonishing good fortune.

Through an unprecedented and almost miraculous turn of events, it was to gain a prominence of which no one in the area in the those early days, could have possibly dreamed.

## Chapter Two

*The Two Brothers — Indian War Paint on the Big Oak Tree —
Forts of Refuge — The Battle of Kings Mountain —
"Alexander Erwin, Lord of the Mountains"*

### 2.

Although the good Bishop Spangenburg came into the piedmont area of North Carolina searching for a place to establish a Moravian settlement in what he termed, "a little corner the Lord has set apart for the brethren," he was not able to find it. It was not until some years later that such a place was discovered in the environs of the present day Winston-Salem. However, there were other pioneers who happily found what they sought.

These early settlers were mostly Scotch-Irish, this nomenclature being bestowed upon them because they were Scotchmen whose forebears had fled from Scotland because of religious and economic persecution and sojourned in Ireland for a time before coming to America, while the others were mainly of English and German extraction.

Among these Scotch-Irish pioneers were two brothers, Arthur and Alexander Erwin, whose family had settled in South Carolina near the present town of York.

On learning that grants of land could be obtained in western North Carolina by men who would settle there, drive out the Indians and colonize the area, they left South Carolina and set forth to try their fortunes in the wilderness of western North Carolina.

Probably, like Bishop Spangenburg, thy came riding into the wilderness following a buffalo trail or an Indian trading path, since there were no other routes to guide them. Skilled in the use of a gun and hunting knife, they must have been continually on the lookout for wild animals and Indians.

The brothers loved the land at first sight, for they were impressed by its richness and beauty and the faraway and majestic Blue Ridge Mountains that towered in the west. This being the case, it was not long before they found the tract they sought. They laid claim upon it and were living on it before the grant to the property had even been completed and before the American Revolution, in which both brothers were to take an active part.

They divided the land between them. Arthur, the older brother, claimed the portion to the north of where the village of Morganton was to be established in future years, and Alexander, the younger brother (1750-1834) took what lay to the northwest, both of them settling on a widespread acreage called Cherryfields, perhaps because of the many wild cherry trees that grew upon it.

From early records we find that not all of these first pioneers were of the ordinary type of settlers. Many were educated, had learned professions and important crafts vital to trading and the expansion of business, and they were seeking a larger theatre in which to enrich themselves and practice the skills they had acquired in their former places of residence.

In fact, we learn that both Arthur Erwin and his brother Alexander Erwin (12 years younger) were educated men who "were widely read". This appears to be true by the prominence they early achieved and by the positions of influence and trust in which they were soon placed.

They obtained land grants, acquired slaves, cultivated plantations along the swift-running rivers and creeks in the fertile upland valleys. As the tide of immigration continued it was only natural that they and men of like accomplishments became the dominant class in the western region of the state. Hard working, energetic and ambitious, it was not long before they established new counties and courts of law, institutions of learning and encouraged a comfortable trade with South Carolina that even reached to Charleston by the sea.

Arthur's son, William W. Erwin, later built a brick house several miles away on Arthur's portion of the property, which he named Belvedere. Tradition tells us that Arthur's father, Nathaniel, who was still living in South Carolina, furnished the money for this home—which probably explains why Arthur is not mentioned in Nathaniel's will.

James, the son of Alexander, the younger brother, later built "a frame house painted white" across the creek about a mile from the home of Alexander on the side of a high hill overlooking the Catawba River and Warrior Creek (now Upper Creek) on property owned by Alexander. Still later, he built a brick house on top of the same hill, which he named Bellevue (after which the "white painted" house was destroyed) and this second house was the home that Silas McDowell described as "a brick mansion above the juncture of Upper Creek and the Catawba River."

Both brothers had large families and many descendants, which in time became so numerous that, in order to distinguish between the

## Chapter Two

two branches of the family, the descendants of Arthur Erwin became known as the Belvidere Erwins, and the descendants of Alexander as the Bellevue Erwins.

My grandfather, Joseph Erwin, the grandson of Alexander Erwin, was given no middle name at birth, but, as he grew older, he began signing his name Joseph J. Erwin. When I was a child and asked what the "J" stood for, I was told he had simply inserted it into his name in order not to be confused with his many cousins who had similar names or initials, and there were times when he even found it necessary to sign himself "Joseph J. Erwin of Bellevue," to keep legal or other records straight.

Nathaniel, the father of Arthur and Alexander, was the first of the family to come to America. He settled in Bucks County, Pennsylvania, then emigrated to North Carolina and lived for a while in what was then Rowan County and also in present-day Mecklenburg County. After this he went on to South Carolina, where he died and was buried, and his will can be seen at the Courthouse in the town of York.

His wife, Leah Julian, was not Scotch, but of Huguenot Protestant descent, a lady of proud heritage. Through the years her surname had been changed to Julian from de St. Julien, and her grandfather, René Julian, was a descendant of the de St. Julien family that had fled from France to escape religious persecution. Some of its prominent members were Pierre de St. Julien, his brother Louis, and their brother-in-law, René Ravenel; all of them wealthy nobility of Vitre in Britagne.

The stories of the two Erwin brothers read much like those of other early pioneers into the piedmont area of North Carolina "who acquired land grants, built homes, and through close planning and hard work became prosperous." Belvedere, the home of Arthur, stood about two miles from Bellevue, the home of Alexander. As the years passed and the descendants of the brothers became more numerous, they retained a close and warm relationship, perhaps due to the inherent love of the clan that seems to be born in the Scotch.

Belvedere caught fire and burned down when I was a girl, but Bellevue still stands at this time (1996), and it is with this old home, where so many of the descendants of Alexander Erwin lived, that a number of stories in this collection of sketches deals.

Much has been written and published about Alexander Erwin. In fact, history books give him high praise and say "he was a remarkable man". We are also told that "his life's story reads more like fiction than truth." Like his older brother, Arthur of Belvedere, he became wealthy and acquired more land until, according to carefully kept family accounts and records, his holdings included twenty thousand acres.

In a collection of old letters the author has found is one that states: "Alexander Erwin was a very prominent man in his day. He was called 'Lord of the Mountains' because of his great influence and the large bodies of land he owned."

At an early age he also became popular and prominent throughout the area. In 1770 when he was twenty years old, he married Sarah Ann Robinson, who was a few months younger than he, and who is still remembered for an act of bravery that caused her death during the Revolution.

She was the daughter of James Harvey Robinson and his wife Catherine Robinson, but unlike the Erwin brothers, who were of Scotch-Irish descent, the Robinson family was of English extraction. They had settled in South Carolina in Lancaster County, and thereby hangs a tale, bloody but interesting, that I never tired of hearing.

It does not begin with the Robinsons, however, but with a German pioneer who built his cabin in an isolated spot deep in the forests of western North Carolina. Near it stood a giant oak tree, a monarch of the forest, that towered above all the trees about it. The man chose that spot, thinking the tree could serve as a landmark to lead him home if he ever went away and became lost.

One day when he was not at home, some hostile Indians who had come into the territory on a hunting expedition, found his home, burned it to the ground and scalped and killed his wife and all of his children. Some friendly Indians in the area told him to leave the place at once because the unfriendly Indians would certainly come back and, if they found him, they would kill him, too. They promised to keep some red Indian war paint smeared on the base of the big oak tree so long as the killer Indians stayed in the environs. They told him he should stay away for as long as it remained, but that if he returned and found no war paint he would know it was safe for him to come back to live there.

The poor grieving man fled southward into South Carolina and was given shelter by the Robinson family. A time came when, on returning to his home place about two years later, he found no war paint on the big oak tree, so he decided to rebuild his cabin and cul-

## Chapter Two

tivate his land. Since he needed help in doing this, he begged one of the Robinson sons to go with him. Young James Harvey Robinson agreed to go, and as time passed the young man became so charmed by the area that he decided to live there, too.

He obtained property along the South Fork River, a tributary of the Catawba River, and he is said to be the "first Englishman to settle in the beautiful South Fork Valley." There he built his home and he and his wife Catherine had a number of children. One of them was named Sarah Ann and she was to grow up and marry young Alexander Erwin, who lived about twenty-five miles away in the Valley of the Catawba on the Cherryfields tract.

Tradition states that the marriage was unusually happy and six children were born to them: James, Catherine, Mary (usually called Pretty Polly), Margaret (called Peggy), Hannah, and Joseph. Their first home stood on the Cherryfields tract on the original land grant to the two brothers, through which ran Warrior Creek (so named because of a fierce battle between Indian tribes in the nearby meadowlands, not far from the juncture of the creek and the Catawba River).

"What sort of house was it?" I asked when I was a child, but no one knew.

"It was probably built of logs like other pioneer homes of that day," surmised an elderly relative who told me the story. "And it probably had gun holes in the walls in case of Indian attacks, for the Indians were roaming freely in the area in those days."

Not far from their home and close to the place where the creek flowed into the river stood one of the Forts of Refuge, to which the settlers could run for safety when the Indians were on the warpath. I was told that certain men were appointed to watch the Indians in an effort to ascertain when they were planning an attack. When this was the case, the Indians would be found working with flint, making and sharpening arrows and tomahawks, and fashioning ax heads and handles. These men who watched the Indians also had the duty of warning the scattered settlers when they thought an attack was about to begin.

Sometimes the attacks came at night and these were especially feared by the settlers. At such times, the watchmen would speed through the darkness on horseback to warn the settlers to flee to a Fort of Refuge. The elderly relative who told me this story recited it with such vivid imagery that I could almost hear the thundering of horses' hooves coming swiftly through the dark; the quick, urgent knocking on doors and the message given in hurried low tones. I could imagine the husband and older sons flinging on some garments and seizing their guns and knives while the wife woke the children, perhaps hushing a crying baby, and then the frightened family running through the darkened forests and meadows to the fort.

One day in the fall of 1780, young Alexander Erwin rode off from home to fight the British at the battle of Kings Mountain, leaving Sarah and the children in the house near Warrior Creek. Both of his saddlebags were filled with corn to feed his horse and himself, if the need should arise, and he probably wore a coat of tanned hide, fringed in the Indian fashion, and homespun trousers—which most of the men who fought with him seem to have worn.

Pinned or sewn to their coonskin caps or hats were insignia indicating their regiments and ranks: a twig of mountain laurel or holly or oak; a small bunch of sumac leaves, red or yellow; or even pieces of white paper cut out in certain shapes. To recognize their horses during the smoke and confusion of battle, they had also dyed the bridles and reins and other trappings on the animals with sumac juice, making them red or yellow.

A Captain of Cavalry, Alexander Erwin probably carried his gun slung over his shoulder by a thong of rawhide. In his belt was a hunting knife, and more than likely, a tomahawk. Dressed in this fashion, he and his fellow patriots made a poor showing when compared with the British soldiers, in their scarlet and white uniforms trimmed with gold lace and gold buttons that gleamed in the autumn sun.

However, each of these valley and mountain men was expert in riding a horse and handling a gun and they knew well the Indian method of guerilla fighting and were eager for battle. Fortunately, in his excitement, Alexander had no inkling of the heart-breaking catastrophe that was to take place at his home after he had gone.

On leaving, Alexander did not go straight to Kings Mountain near the border between North and South Carolina. The designated meeting place was in the grassy low-lying meadowland, called Quaker Meadows, along the Catawba River on the property of Charles McDowell, which adjoined Alexander's lands. In these widespread meadows stood a huge old oak tree, later called the Council Oak, under the spreading branches of which the men gathered to plan their battle strategy. It was still standing when I was a child, but was washed away by the flood of 1916 when I was seven years old.

The patriots of western North Carolina, knowing they were no match in numbers or in equipment to strike against the British, had sent word for help over the mountains to the "over mountain men" (as they have been called ever since that time), who had quickly agreed to come to their aid.

Following Indian trails and pressing on through hazardous mountain passes, they travelled as speedily as possible from Tennessee, Kentucky and what is now West Virginia; and, although it is only natural that there should be a few contradictions recorded in the confusion of the fighting at Kings Mountain, it appears to be certain that at least a thousand "good, hardy and trusty men" came to join the waiting western North Carolina men at Quaker Meadows in the Valley of the Catawba.

The local men, led by Joseph McDowell, naturally assumed that he would take command of the collected forces, but there were others who thought he was too old a man to lead such an arduous expedition. Their discussions caused some delay, so a man had to be sent on horseback to the General Assembly, then sitting in Hillsborough, North Carolina, to get it to settle the matter, and William Campbell of West Virginia was appointed to take command.

Worried by the thought of their delay, they were determined to press on in spite of the cold, soaking rain that had begun to fall. They knew that the British General Ferguson had already stationed his troops on the top of Kings Mountain, declaring he was "king of the mountain and only the Lord Himself could drive him from it." All night long the patriots paced their horses through the darkness and the steady rain, and at about three o'clock on the morning of October 7, 1780, after being in the saddle thirty hours without rest, and drenched by the heavy rain, they reached and surrounded Kings Mountain.

Simultaneously and without delay, they ascended the mountain on all sides and began their attack. The battle was "fierce, furious, and bloody," and the record states that "the whole mountain was covered with smoke and seemed to thunder."

General Ferguson rode a beautiful white horse and signaled to his troops on a silver whistle with a peculiarly piercing note as he galloped back and forth upon the mountain top, which enabled the patriots to ascertain his position at all times. As a result, he was killed and the battle that turned the tide of the Revolutionary War in the South was won by the men of western North Carolina and the "over mountain men" of Tennessee, Kentucky, and West Virginia.

Later on, when these courageous guerilla fighters turned homeward after the victory at Kings Mountain, they must have been filled with excitement, joy and pride over what they had accomplished.

As for Alexander Erwin, when he reached his home and found an almost unbearable tragedy awaiting him there, his exhilarating emotions were quickly changed to shock and horror and a grief that never healed—which he was known to carry in his heart for the rest of his life.

## Chapter Three

*A Tragic Death —
The Log Courthouse with a Whipping Post and Stocks—
Pretty Polly's Son*

### 3.

Not long after Alexander Erwin rode off to fight the British at Kings Mountain on that autumn day in 1780, his young wife, Sarah, looked out across the bottom lands along the river and saw a neighbor man running rapidly toward her home. He had been wounded by some Tories, by whom he was being pursued, and he said they would surely kill him if they caught him; so he begged her to hide him as quickly as she could.

Under the influence of the British General Ferguson, who had briefly entered the North Carolina mountains, these Tories had sided with the English king and gathered into bands, their object being to capture and even to kill every patriot they could find. Aware of this, Sarah Erwin, in the stress of the moment, tried to find the safest place to hide him, and she placed him in the weave house, a small building at the rear of her home where cloth was woven. She hid him under a large pile of woven cloth just before a Tory officer and several men arrived. They demanded that she give up the man she was hiding, and when she refused, they searched every corner of the house and even ran their bayonets into the feather beds.

Not finding him, they began a search of the other buildings on the place. When they reached the weave house, Sarah tried to stop them, but the Tory officer quickly thrust her aside, his unsheathed sword in his hand, saying sharply, "Stand aside!" He and his men entered the building, and, as he approached the place where the victim was hiding, Sarah stepped forward instinctively and flung her arm over the pile of woven cloth in an attempt to save the man.

Quick though she was, the descending blade of the sword of the Tory officer, who it is said did not mean to kill her, struck her in the side of the neck and made an horrendous gash down across her shoulder and breast, leaving her covered with blood and lying senseless on the floor, close to death. Amazingly, she survived, but the wound became infected and it was from this she died several years later at the age of thirty-five, her death continuing to be a terrible memory for Alexander the rest of his life.

The man whose life Sarah Robinson Erwin attempted to save was not killed, but for the rest of his days he bore a scar on his forehead from the Tory officer's sword and he often told how he had received it. How he escaped I never asked, for I was so horrified over the ghastly story.

Alexander married again, but the elderly relative who told me the tale always added with emphasis, "He never forgot or ceased to love Sarah and he requested that when he died, he be buried by her side."

Alexander's second wife, a Mrs. Margaret Patton, had children of her own and was evidently a neighbor, for when Alexander rode home from the battle of Kings Mountain, he brought to her, tied to his saddle, the horse of her husband, Joseph Patton, who died during the fighting. In those hard early days he obviously needed a wife to run his home and to help care for his children, and she needed a husband to fend for her and her offspring.

Catherine, the daughter of Alexander and his young first wife, Sarah, married her first cousin John Erwin, the son of her uncle Arthur Erwin of Belvedere, and a tragedy befell them when all their children died about the same time from a contagious disease. The couple was so grief stricken that they sold their land and moved to Georgia, where they were blessed in having the same number of children that had died in North Carolina.

Margaret (called Peggy) married Hugh Tate, a member of a prominent family in the area. Hannah married Zebulon Baird. She moved with him into the mountains near the present city of Asheville and became the ancestress of North Carolina's beloved Governor Zebulon Baird Vance. Mary (called Pretty Polly) married the Reverend John McCamey Wilson, minister of the first Presbyterian church in Quaker Meadows. She has been confused in some records with her first cousin, the daughter of her uncle Arthur Erwin, who was also named Mary and used the nickname Polly, which was popular at the time—at which one may surmise that Pretty Polly was really the prettier of the two.

Be that as it may be, Polly, the daughter of Arthur Erwin, married a man by the name of Joseph Patton (who is sometimes confused with the Joseph Patton whose widow became the second wife of Alexander Erwin) and they had a son named Arthur for her father, Arthur Erwin, whose son William W. Erwin, built Belvedere.

Pretty Polly, the daughter of Alexander Erwin who married the young minister, John McCamey Wilson, had a number of children, mostly sons. One of them, named Alexander Erwin Wilson, wanted to go to Africa as a missionary, but he discovered that the Presbyterian church would not allow him to do this unless he had a wife. He therefore advertised for a wife in a church periodical and a young lady from Richmond, Virginia, wrote to him that her dearest wish was to be a missionary to Africa.

She turned out to be well born, pious, and satisfactory in every way. They met, found they were congenial and sailed for Africa not long before the Civil War. Unfortunately, the place to which they were sent had a bad climate and was inhabited by head-hunters and cannibals, but they continued to live there for a time until a daughter was born. While the child was still an infant the mother died, and the grieving young husband, fearing his wife's remains might be molested by the head-hunters and cannibals, secretly dug her grave himself in the jungle at night.

Into her grave he put a piece of soapstone on which he had carved her name and the dates of her birth and death. Then he camouflaged the grave as well as he was able and decided to leave the area, being too brokenhearted to remain longer in that place.

Learning that a ship would be sailing soon to the United States, he made arrangements with the captain of the vessel to take the baby to her mother's relatives in Richmond, Virginia. Then he got in touch with the famous missionary to Africa, Dr. David Livingston, and went to work with him at his mission, where he died at the age of twenty-nine.

Many years later the British government began work on a railroad in the Transvaal of Africa and the wife's grave was upturned. The piece of soapstone with her name and dates upon it was found. It was taken to the British Museum in London, where it remained while an investigation concerning it was carried out.

At length, after a number of years had passed, the mystery was solved. By then the daughter had grown up and had children of her own. These children, when grown, began a search for the relatives of their grandfather, who had been the young missionary Alexander Erwin Wilson, and they found and met his relatives, a few of whom were living in Charlotte, North Carolina.

Joseph Erwin, the second son of Alexander Erwin, moved to South Carolina and died unmarried, but James Erwin, the elder of the two sons, married Margaret Locke Phifer, the daughter of Colonel Martin Phifer, Jr. Colonel Martin Phifer, Jr. was a wealthy planter whose plantation, called Coldwater, was situated in the area of the present town of Concord, North Carolina. He was a member of the Provincial Congress, held many important offices, and a published record tells us that at one time he was the largest landowner in the state. He took a conspicuous part in the War of the Revolution and played a dangerous role in carrying messages from General Washington to the North Carolina troops.

His wife, Margaret Locke Phifer, was the granddaughter of General Matthew Locke, who was also conspicuous for his services in the Revolutionary War, as was his brother Colonel Francis Locke. Colonel Locke, also a man of prominence, was killed at the battle of Charlotte close to Sugaw Creek Presbyterian Church. Their younger brother Major George Locke, only nineteen years old, was killed at Cowan's Ford. Both died close to the same time during the war.

In recorded history, we read that General Matthew Locke was "greatly respected and admired by all who knew him, was known especially for his integrity and should have had a Boswell, as did Samuel Johnson, to write about his many accomplishments." However, lacking such a biographer, "he has not received the full amount of acclaim that was his due"; for it is surprising that in the span of one life he could have held so many offices and accomplished so much.

General Matthew Locke and his brother, Francis Locke, lived about four miles from Salisbury, North Carolina and ran a line of covered Conestoga wagons to Charleston, that carried local products that were shipped abroad, mainly to England. These "were mostly deer, bear, mink, otter and beaver skins, for at that time the trade in pelts was immense and very lucrative."

They also brought back supplies that had been carried by ships to Charleston and through these activities they became prosperous. A note in an old ledger at the Moravian settlement at Winston-Salem states, "The Lockes' wagons have arrived with supplies," but the would-be buyer demurred "at the high prices that are charged."

General Matthew Locke became prominent not only in his state but throughout the nation as well. He was a member of the Provincial Congress and also of the Congress of the United States (from 1773 to 1799). He served with distinction in the War of the Revolution and was a religious man, being a vestryman for many years at Saint Luke's Episcopal Church in Salisbury.

In 1784, a few years after the Battle of Kings Mountain, Alexander Erwin was appointed, along with Charles McDowell and James Blanton, "to lay out a village on high ground near the Catawba River in the newly established County of Burke (formed from Rowan

County) and to build there a courthouse and a jail, and to erect a whipping post and stocks."

The new county was named for North Carolina's Governor Burke, and according to the record, Alexander Erwin was appointed to this honor because of "his meritorious services at Kings Mountain, Cowpens, and other battles of the Revolutionary War."

Some of the streets of Morganton were named for streets in Charleston, South Carolina—among them King, Sterling, and Union Streets. From its early days, the little village had an interesting link with Charleston, which became its egress to the sea and its port of entrance. There, ships from England, France, and other foreign countries were increasingly dropping anchor, not only bringing news from the outside world but articles of all sorts to be sold in the village as the villagers' tastes became more sophisticated with the passing of time.

Alexander Erwin was made the first Justice of the Court of Pleas and Quarter Sessions and the first Clerk of the County Court, in Morganton, which were high positions in that day, and he held them for many years—until his son, James Erwin, succeeded him. Joseph J. Erwin, the son of James, succeeded James—Alexander, James and Joseph occupying these same offices consecutively for sixty-eight years.

After the Revolutionary War, hatred continued for many years between the patriots and the Tories, so quarrelling and fighting sometimes broke out between them in Morganton, disturbing the peace. Because of these outbreaks, during his term of office, Alexander Erwin would allow no Tory to come into the village except on matters of business. Nor would he allow a Tory to remain in town overnight. However, some people claimed that one of the real reasons for this was his hostility toward the Tories because of the brutal wounding and subsequent death of his beloved first wife, Sarah Robinson Erwin, at the hand of the Tory officer.

Family tradition tells us that every afternoon when Alexander left his office at the Courthouse, he would ride his horse about the Courthouse Square, shake his riding crop above his head, and shout, "Every Tory leave the town! Every Tory leave the town!"—an order that was speedily obeyed.

Although we find a great deal about Alexander Erwin in early histories of North Carolina, we have no description of his physical appearance. We learn that he was "an outstanding man, popular and highly respected by others," which is supported by the many high positions and offices of trust he occupied.

We also learn that he was religious and was a Ruling Elder at the little Presbyterian Church in Quaker Meadows near Morganton. Since the elderly lady manager of the inn at Morganton told the newcomer, Silas McDowell, that Alexander Erwin was "a great reader of books," it was not unusual that he was interested in education and was one of the founders and trustees of the Morgan Academy, the first institution of learning in Burke County.

He represented Burke County a number of times in the Provincial Congress and in 1784, when the village of Morganton was incorporated under the name of Town of Morgan, he was made one of the three District Auditors for the counties of Burke, Lincoln, Sullivan, Washington, and Wilkes. In this position he was "vested with full powers and authority to finally settle and adjust all claims against the state for military pay and for all articles which have been or may be purchased for the use of the state." It was because of this high honor that the rank of Colonel was bestowed upon him.

In history books we read that he was "a brave and energetic soldier, serving as an officer in the Revolutionary War, a statesman and a member of the Provincial Congress, that he was popular and highly respected by those who knew him and that he dispensed a gracious hospitality at his home, as did his brother Arthur."

He was gregarious and sociable, enjoying the company of his friends and liking to gather with them. He also appreciated music, and a story that is not found in a history book but has been handed down by his descendants, states that he played skillfully upon the flute. This musical instrument is today in the possession of one of his descendants.

One account of him says that he was "intelligent, honest, and dependable, a stout-hearted old hero of the pronounced Whig type who died rich in many honors and was an ornament to his country." He outlived his first wife Sarah Ann Robinson Erwin by many years and his obituary in the newspaper may throw still more light on his character and personality:

### OBITUARY OF ALEXANDER ERWIN
June 6, 1750 - June 20, 1829

... Died at his residence Cherryfields in Burke County on the 16th instant, Colonel Alexander Erwin, aged 80 years - 8 months - 4 days. One of the few remaining patriots of 1775—who supported and maintained the glorious cause of American Liberty in the times of perilous trust in the War of the Revolution. He was distinguished through life by a peculiar suavity of address, for his innate hospitality, love and charity to man, especially to the bereaved and helpless. Gifted with a firm, athletic constitution, he scarcely knew sickness or pain until far advanced in the evening of life; when it came, he bore it with exemplary patience and resignation, and in the end went off without a struggle or groan—leaving behind a numerous and respectable family connection to regret their loss and to appreciate his worth—but consoled with comfortable hopes that the latter part is committed to a House not made with hands, eternal in the heavens.[1]

He was buried beside his first wife, Sarah Robinson Erwin, as he had requested, and the two have slept together through the long years in the little Presbyterian cemetery on a low hill in Quaker Meadows just across the Catawba River from Morganton.

Never have I seen two gravestones standing so close together. It almost appears that Sarah's grave was widened, so that his casket could be placed as close as possible to hers, and we are touched also by a certain poignancy in the words on Sarah's gravestone, beneath which her wounded and maimed body has rested for so long:

MEMENTO MORI

In Memory of Sarah Erwin
Who Departed This Life 1785, aged 35 Years,
An Affectionate Wife and Tender Mother

*When I lie buried deep in dust*
*My flesh shall be Thy care,*
*These with'ring limbs with Thee I trust*
*To raise them fresh and fair.*

---

[1] Although June 6, 1750 is accepted as the date of Alexander Erwin's birth, there seems to be some confusion among historians as to the date of his death (June 20, 1829, as shown on his gravestone, or June 20, 1830, that is often cited), but when the years, months and days of his life shown on his gravestone are examined, the date appears to be February 10, 1834.

*The Halcyon Years — The Discovery of Gold (1839 - 1840) — The Supreme Court of North Carolina — Why Morganton Was Called "The Gem In The Wilderness"*

### 4.

James Erwin (1775-1848), the son of Colonel Alexander Erwin and his wife Sarah Ann Robinson Erwin, was born to a life of much more ease and comfort than his father, the pioneer.

He spent his childhood and youth at the home of his parents, which stood on a portion of the original land grant to his father and his uncle Arthur Erwin that was called Cherryfields and was close to Warrior Creek (now Upper Creek), not far from the place where the creek flows into the Catawba River.

James Erwin, like his father Alexander Erwin, took an active part in public affairs, representing his county in the Provincial Congress and holding other positions of importance. He also succeeded his father in the office of Justice of the Court of Pleas and Quarter Sessions and Clerk of the Court at Morganton, but attention to business matters, rather than to politics, was his first interest.

A published record states that he was "a shrewd and apt businessman, far-seeing in his plans and by ceaseless industry coupled with good judgement and a quiet tongue, he acquired a large property in land and slaves and was devoted to his wife and children and patriotic after the old Roman pattern." According to well kept family records, he possessed an estate that extended from near Morganton for ten miles to the northwest.

He is described as being "a man of fine presence, six feet tall with a fair complexion, hazel eyes, and brown hair with a glint of red"— which can be seen in a portrait owned by one of his descendants. When I was a child and asked an elderly lady who had known him what he was like, she spoke of his fine appearance and his courtly manners, adding that she had always noticed, "the grace and ease with which he moved and deported himself at a dancing party." When I asked the same question of an elderly gentleman who had known him, his reply was quite different.

"James Erwin," he said, "was the most amazingly winded man I have ever known. He was as strong as a bull, as lithe as an Indian, and as quick as a cat. He became known for his remarkable physical strength and he never met a man he could not throw."

I learned from this same gentleman that in those early days, "young men often went about to fairs and 'in-gatherings' to test their strength in physical contests with other men." The unusual strength of James Erwin became so well-known that men sometimes came not only from North Carolina but from other states as well to engage him in contests of strength, and he never lost a bout.

His wife, Margaret Locke Phifer, whom he married on January 7, 1808, was the daughter of Colonel Martin Phifer, Jr., a large landowner and a member of the Provincial Congress. She was also a granddaughter of General Matthew Locke, who was one of the prominent men of the state. Thus, according to the record, she, like James, was "well endowed in purse" and, according to family tradition, also "well endowed in person."

From her father she had inherited a large amount of land in Tennessee, and James, who was known as "a superb horseman who could ride like the wind," sometimes went alone on long horseback rides, changing horses along the way, over the mountains into Tennessee to look after his wife's property. His unusual endurance and horsemanship was a source of amazement to those who knew him, since he could make the trips more quickly than any other man had been known to make such long, tiring, and hazardous rides.

His incredible strength, coordination and energy must have stayed with him well through the years, for after he was married and had seven children, these attributes were tested by guests at a social gathering at his home, Bellevue. In the dining room there was a sideboard that was larger and higher off the floor than most, and some of his guests made a bet that he could not leap to its top without first taking a running start.

On one of his trips over the mountains to Tennessee he had encountered a group of Indians from whom he bought a pair of beaded moccasins of the softest doeskin. He put on these moccasins, had the top of the sideboard cleared, took a few steps forward and leapt easily to its top, where, to the delight of all, he danced a "short, Indian-like jig."

What seemed quite remarkable to me when I heard the tale was that when he leapt and while he danced, he held a glass of wine in his hand and he did not spill a drop. When I asked an elderly maiden aunt, who was abstemious about this, it was obvious that she wished that part of the story were left out—for she answered reluctantly that there were some persons who said that happened.

At the time of his marriage to Margaret Locke Phifer, James built a home on the side of a high hill across Warrior Creek from his childhood home on the Cherryfields tract, where his father Alexander Erwin was still living. When I asked about this house, no one seemed to know much about it except that it was built of wood, painted white and was commodious enough to house comfortably the children who were born to him and Margaret while they lived there.

Their children included five boys and two girls: William Crawford, Joseph, Martin Phifer, George Washington, Alexander, Elizabeth Phifer, and Sarah Ann. While the children were still young, James built a home of brick on the top of the hill (on the side of which the white frame house stood).

The new home (1823) he named Bellevue because of the beautiful views of the valley and the mountains that surrounded it. James Erwin, by then a wealthy planter, wanted a home in keeping with his more prosperous mode of life. The bricks for his new home on the hilltop were made by his slaves from clay on the place, and the frame house just down the hill was demolished.

For the lime for the brick work and for other necessities, James sent slaves in wagons to Charleston under the supervision of his overseer, the lime having been brought to Charleston as ballast in ships that anchored there. Hand blown glass for the windows and other embellishments for the house that could not be found in the Morganton area were also brought from Charleston.

The new home was two stories tall with an attic above, and a basement below containing a wine cellar and a workroom. On the east, there was a one story wing containing two bedrooms with a long one story porch behind them. In front of the major portion of the house were tall white columns, two stories in height with two porches, one above the other in the Charleston manner, and at the rear, behind the parlor, was a porch with two-story white columns. The parlor and the bedroom above it were quite large. The ceilings in all rooms were unusually high and every room had its own fireplace.

On the side lawn to the west an office was built, where James could attend to business, keep plantation records and confer with his overseer who "rode his acres for him, looked after his lands and managed his slaves."

The office was built of the same brick as the house. It had white trim and contained two large rooms, one above and one below. A white painted stair climbed the outside east wall of the office and it was by this that one reached the second floor. The second floor room was furnished as a bedroom and contained several double beds, for

## Chapter Four

it served as a dormitory for the boys of the family when there was an overflow of guests in the home. This building, which was attractive and went well with the home, was standing when I was a child but was later torn down.

Because of the danger of fires in that day, a kitchen, which was made of brick, stood apart from and to the rear of the house. It had four rooms; the two below serving as a cooking room and store room, the two above as quarters for the cook. A well under a small white painted structure with a peaked roof stood close to the back door, but James, having an inventive turn of mind, had hit upon a plan to have another source of fresh, clean water at his new home that must have been an astonishment to all who knew of it.

On a nearby hill he had discovered a fine spring of water, which he managed to transport to Bellevue through bored hickory logs, ingeniously fastened together and laid underground till they reached the house; and this unusual water system, which ran continuously day and night, served for many years before I was born, until the logs rotted or came apart with age.

Not far from the kitchen stood several houses for the house servants. There was a smokehouse nearby and also an ice house. In the latter, the ice, cut from the ice ponds constructed on the place, was stored for use in the summer months, and the building was set so deeply in the ground that one had to descend some steps to reach it. It was round in shape and had a peaked roof, which was the only part of it that could be seen above ground. It also had an inner and outer wall between which straw was kept closely packed. Unfortunately, this interesting structure had been done away with before I was old enough to visit at Bellevue, for by that time, ice was being hauled from town, cut in big blocks, in the enclosed back of an ice wagon drawn by a mule, and all that was left of the ice house was a sunken place in the grassy back yard.

A little farther from the back of the house was the Necessary House, which was reminiscent of those at George Washington's Mount Vernon, but a little larger, and at Bellevue it was called "the Garden House." It could be reached by a walk of large flat rocks that led to it from the back porch and it stood behind a thick hedge of tall fig bushes that hid it completely. Unlike the house, which was of brick with white trimmings, it was painted a dull, dark grey, which, I was told, was to "make it more inconspicuous."

To lay out his grounds and gardens, James Erwin employed an English landscape gardener named Melton, who planted boxwoods brought from England, constructed walkways, and arranged areas for flower and vegetable gardens, grape arbors, and orchards.

The flower gardens were at the foot of the sloping front lawn and enclosed in four square sections surrounded by boxwoods with a walkway that made an aisle between two rows of boxwoods down the center of the whole garden. Lower still were terraces, where a large variety of vegetables and herbs were grown, and there were several levels of strawberry beds, while below these was a large area for different types of berry bushes and several grape arbors.

This arrangement was still in use when I was a child, except that one side of the original boxwood-enclosed flower gardens had disappeared. This occurred when the meadows in the bottom lands in front of and below the house were being burned off, as was done from time to time in those days. The flames had gotten out of control, swept up the hill toward the house and destroyed the boxwoods and gardens on the east side. This fire occurred after the Civil War when times were hard and money was scarce, so the boxwoods and gardens on that side were not replaced, and have not been until this day (1996), although much of the symmetry and beauty of the gardens was lost.

Margaret and James Erwin inherited some of the furniture they put in their home at Bellevue. Some was brought by ship from England to Charleston and then transported to Bellevue by wagon. Other pieces were made by skilled Swiss furniture makers who were touring the South at that time, stopping at plantations along the way and making furniture. They stayed for a year at Bellevue, camping in the bottom lands.

Sons and daughters were continually getting married on the various Southern plantations and moving away to homes of their own; so new furniture was always needed. Often masters and mistresses of the plantations wanted replacements of worn out pieces or wished for new pieces made according to ideas and whims of their own—following the design of the legs on certain chairs but using different arms and backs, etc.

These pieces of furniture, made according to the plantation owners' ideas, were called "plantation pieces," and can be seen in homes throughout the South today. The Swiss furniture makers usually used wood from locally grown trees, saved and cured for this work. They brought their own satinwood for inlay work or used maple wood from trees on the plantations. These pieces were beautifully made and, of course, had considerable sentimental value.

## Chapter Four

The years that James and Margaret Phifer Erwin lived at Bellevue could be called the Halcyon Years—the years of prosperity, of ease, comfort, and plenty—when there was no indication of the heartbreak, poverty and tragedy that the Civil War was to bring to Bellevue, as to the whole South. It is of this period before the war that Governor Zebulon Vance wrote in his "Sketches of North Carolina" (1875):

"The richness and beauty of the Catawba Valley made it the most attractive in the state; and at an early date, not later than 1760, it was filled with settlers of the best type, principally Scotch-Irish and English with a sprinkling of Dutch (Germans). They seized upon the fertile river bottoms and the lowlands of the many tributaries of the Catawba and laid the foundation for the wealth and comfort for many thousands of their descendants. The principal settlers were the Averys, Erwins, Tates, Forneys, Pearsons, Lytles, Connellys, Caldwells, Lenoirs, Greenlees, Burgins, Carsons—and many others who cannot be named in so short a sketch as this. All of them were active and zealous participators in the Indian Wars or in the struggle of the Revolution.

"Such could not fail to make good citizens in peace and excellent society. In fact, that valley region in time became the seat of culture and refinement in western North Carolina and today it maintains its high reputation in that respect. No portion of our state better illustrated the country life which so much resembled that of the British. The land was filled with well-to-do gentlemen with ample estates well stocked with flocks and herds that fed upon the rich mountain pastures in summer and were cared for upon the meadows of the lowlands in winter. Slavery in a truly patriarchal form flourished among them, the servants constituting a much regarded and protected part of every gentleman's family.

"The little village of Morganton was the center around which their homes were located. Close by flowed the fresh, rapid Catawba and thickly over the bold uplands stood the seats of these gentlemen farmers, the smoke from whose chimneys rose upon the pure, transparent atmosphere as a sign of hospitality and good cheer. Rounds of visiting by whole families, with horses, carriages and servants, lasting for days and weeks was the fashion. Pleasure was a serious and engrossing business. And why not? It was literally a land of abundance."

Governor Vance ends his sketch by saying:

> "They were admirable specimens of the old-time Southern country gentlemen—upright, scornful of mean things, shrewd and intelligent, lovers of liberty and good government, domineering, hospitable, charitable, kindly, and courageous."

James Erwin died many years before his wife, Margaret Phifer Erwin, so my aunts, Mary Louise and Elizabeth Matilda, who were his grandchildren and whom I visited often at Bellevue when they were elderly ladies and I was a child, did not know him as well as they did his wife, their grandmother. They were very fond as well as proud of her, and told me that, "Grandma was rich, an heiress in her own right." They also said that, "Grandma was so proud she'd hardly put her foot to the ground." She never let her grandchildren forget that they were descended from Pfeiffer Von Heisselburg of the German nobility whose descendants had migrated to Switzerland, where they held high positions and later left to come to America in 1737.

In spite of her pride, she was said to be a "kind, merry, talkative, and friendly old lady who was popular with everyone and highly respected by all who knew her." I was also told that she was "active, spritely, small and slim," and always meticulously groomed. She wore "long, black silk dresses that reached the floor and were made in the old-fashioned style," and on her head there was always a white cap, spotless and carefully starched, which was the fashion with elderly ladies of her day.

When gold was discovered in the Morganton area (about 1838-40), James Erwin began mining operations on land he owned in nearby Rutherford County. It is interesting to note that the gold that was first mined near Morganton was discovered by a stranger who was passing through the area and noticed that the clay chinking between the logs of a certain cabin glistened oddly. On learning that the clay came from a nearby creek, he spoke to the owner of the cabin and both men went to work, secretly panning for gold.

Their discovery could not be hidden for long. Soon the streets of

## Chapter Four

Morganton were swarming with miners from other places, eager to mine for gold. As the news spread, wealthy men, the "landed gentry" from the great cotton and tobacco plantations in the coastal region of North Carolina, Virginia, and South Carolina, became interested and many of them flocked to the village to speculate in mining operations. Often they brought with them sons, relatives, and friends who were also interested in mining, and it was estimated that soon about five thousand slaves that they had brought with them were engaged in mining in the area.

For a few years mining continued at a rapid rate, bringing the village of Morganton to the attention of the entire state, as well as other states, and before long it was being referred to as "The Gem in the Wilderness"; for according to the record, more gold was mined in the Morganton area than anywhere else in the nation at that time. Surprisingly, the gold was a soft yellow color, a different hue from gold found elsewhere, which added interest to the undertaking, and a mint for assaying the precious metal was quickly built.

To accommodate the influx of newcomers, a large and handsome hotel was erected in the center of town across from the Courthouse, and "dances and other entertainments were held there every night." Several churches that also served as public meeting places were built and a race track was established in Quaker Meadows just across the river. (It is interesting to note that James Erwin of Bellevue owned a well-known race horse named Melody that he often raced for good sized purses.) Naturally, with so much going on and so much new litigation, the court at Morganton began to flounder under a load of work that it was not equipped to handle, and the state awoke to the fact that it needed help if justice was to be dispensed.

Accordingly, the North Carolina State Legislature (in its session of 1846-47) decided that the State Supreme Court, seated at the capital in Raleigh, should leave the capital and move to the village "on the first day of August yearly and for every year thereafter for the trying of cases and remain there so long as needed."

By that time, the village had already gained in importance for being the only town in the state that was "born a court town," having been established for the express purpose of serving as the county seat of a new county (Burke). The coming of the Supreme Court gave it still more prestige, since no other town in the state, and in so far as we can find, no town in any other state, had this distinction bestowed upon it.

Added to this was the discovery of gold, which made it a still more important and well-known place. The lengthy visits of the "landed gentry" from the great plantations in the eastern part of the state of South Carolina and Virginia, who came there to mine and speculate in gold, gave the villagers and planters the opportunity to rub shoulders with wealthy and sophisticated persons, which lent much to the area's development.

When the Chief Justice of the Supreme Court and all the associate justices began journeying to the village every year for a lengthy stay, they brought their families with them to enjoy the fresh mountain breezes, the healthy climate and the beautiful scenery. Well-known lawyers from other towns who had cases at the court also journeyed there and often they, too, brought along their families for a holiday. State officials, clerks, and other persons working with the legislature, as well as young lawyers wishing to be licensed there, came also, and with them flocks of hangers-on, some wanting to see the prominent persons on hand and others coming simply out of curiosity to find out what was going on.

Over the years, the mule-drawn wagons from Charleston had come in increasing numbers, rumbling up the dirt road to the village, bringing more expensive and sophisticated merchandise than in the past: Paris bonnets, Morocco slippers, silks, satins, velvets and laces for the ladies; and for the gentlemen, beaver and silk top hats, fine gold watches, embroidered vests and silk and linen handkerchiefs— which articles can be seen listed today in an old ledger book of a store in the village.

Naturally, the many strangers attracted to the town for various reasons brought a quickened pace and an added sophistication, and those who came were surprised to find that "the little Gem in the Wilderness constituted a small paradise of sorts of which they had been unaware." From its contact with Charleston, the town had learned much during the years and the wealthy planters, especially the landed gentry from the east, were surprised to find in Morganton, "in spite of its smallness and isolation, a pleasant and congenial society in which they could feel at home."

They were also surprised to find in the village and the surrounding valley a number of large and handsome homes. As this became more widely known, it was only natural that sons and young male relatives and friends of planters—as well as other wellborn persons—attracted by the climate, the rich soil, the scenery, and the pleasant social life, decided to settle in the once obscure but prospering little village that was becoming known as "the center of culture and aristocracy in the western part of the state."

James and Margaret Phifer Erwin were fortunate in living in these halcyon days, and not having to endure the vicissitudes relative to pioneer times and the Revolutionary War. Their only tragedy of which we know was the death of their young son, Alexander Erwin, who contracted what was then called "brain fever" while he was a student at West Point. When he became ill, his black body servant started with him to Bellevue, "to take him to his mother," but he grew worse on the way and they had to stop at Salisbury at the home of relatives, the Crawfords, where he died at the age of nineteen. The weather was warm, and, due to the difficulty of transporting a body any distance at such a time, he was buried in the Crawford burial plot.

The helmet he had worn as a cadet at West Point was kept in a certain cabinet at Bellevue, and sometimes my aunt Mary Louise Erwin, who lived at Bellevue with her sister Elizabeth Matilda, would take it out, show it to me and tell me about her young uncle Alexander Erwin, who had worn it long ago at West Point. At such times she always said, "At least, he was buried with his kindred," and in this thought she appeared to take comfort.

When a Presbyterian church was built in Morganton, James and Margaret Phifer Erwin joined it and became regular attendants. James Erwin died in 1848 at the age of seventy-three. Margaret outlived him many years, and now both sleep together in the cemetery of the First Presbyterian Church in Morganton.

Liking people and being of a gregarious nature, Margaret became lonely after the death of James, with only the servants to keep her company, so she decided to divide her holdings and possessions amongst her children and to invite one of them to live with her. To her sons, George Washington and Martin Phifer, she gave lands in Tennessee and they went there to live.

Her son Joseph was supervising the gold mining activities on land owned by his father in Rutherford County, for James Erwin had sent Joseph and his bride, Elvira Jane Holt, there directly after their marriage.

Her eldest son, William Crawford Erwin, was living in a large and handsome home, (built with part of his inheritance) in town next to the Courthouse between Green and Sterling Streets.

Her older daughter, Elizabeth Phifer, had married the Honorable Burton Craige of Salisbury, North Carolina and had gone there to live, and her younger daughter, Sarah Ann, had married Dr. John

McDowell, her cousin, who was a descendant of Arthur Erwin of the Belvedere branch of the family. Sarah Ann had inherited a large portion of land on the Cherryfields tract, overlooking John's River, from her father James Erwin, and had built a home she called Ash Hill because of the many ash trees upon it.

After Margaret's affairs were settled and she had divided her holdings as fairly as she was able, it was her second son Joseph whom she chose to come to Bellevue. She told him that if he would bring his family to Bellevue, run the place and look after her until she died, she would leave him the plantation and the house on the hilltop, (but certain furnishings of the house she would divide among her other children).

While Joseph and Elvira were living in Rutherford County, where Joseph managed the gold mining activities of his father, three little girls had been born to them. The eldest, my Aunt Mary Lou, told me she remembered well the day they moved to Bellevue. She was five years old and she recalled the long, tiring ride through the mountains. They came in a closed carriage, with their furniture and belongings following in wagons, and went first to the home of their uncle William Erwin, which stood next to the Courthouse on the east between Green and Sterling Streets. Their grandmother had come to town to greet them and when the carriage drew up before the house, she was standing at the front door, eagerly awaiting their arrival.

Aunt Mary Lou even remembered what her grandmother Margaret was wearing—a long black silk dress of old-fashioned design and a white cap on her head. She said that, at sight of them, the old lady "threw up her hands and exclaimed with joy." Her Uncle William Erwin urged them all to stay for a visit, but they were weary after their long journey and eager to get to Bellevue. So her grandmother got into the carriage with them and rode to the old home, "laughing and talking all the way." After their move to Bellevue, a fourth little girl was born. She was named Corinna Morehead, and was the first child of the family to be born at Bellevue.

Joseph's wife, Elvira Jane Holt, a daughter of Dr. William Rainey Holt of Lexington, North Carolina, had received her education at Edgeworth Female Academy in Greensboro, North Carolina. At the academy, she had roomed with her cousin and best friend, Corinna Morehead, the daughter of Governor John M. Morehead. The two girls were related through the Harper family line, both of them being descendants of General Jeduthan Harper. Corinna Morehead mar-

## Chapter Four

ried William Waighstill Avery of Morganton, who was a cousin of Joseph J. Erwin of Bellevue, and it was at their wedding festivities that Elvira Holt and Joseph Erwin met.

Both Elvira and Joseph were attendants in Corinna's wedding, but in those days they were called "waiters," being said to "wait upon the bride and groom." Elvira told her daughters that she and Joseph Erwin met on the dance floor at a ball given in honor of Corinna Morehead and she thought Joseph was the handsomest man she had ever seen.

After their wedding, Corinna Morehead and William Waighstill Avery moved to Morganton to live. Several years later Joseph Erwin and Elvira Holt married and moved to Rutherford County and then to Bellevue, at which time the cousins resumed their friendly relationship of the past and remained close friends for the rest of their lives. The road from Bellevue to Morganton ran in front of the Avery home, which stood to the west of the Courthouse near the center of town, so the Erwin carriage often stopped there en route to and from town, and the daughters of the two families visited each other and got together at social festivities.

When Joseph's mother, Margaret Phifer Erwin, was old, she became blind from cataracts, for which there was no cure in that day. I was told that, in spite of her blindness, she never lost her sunny, cheerful disposition and was always a pleasant, kind, thoughtful and happy person while living at Bellevue with her son, Joseph, her daughter-in-law, Elvira Holt Erwin, and her numerous grandchildren.

The love that my father, his sisters, and brothers (the offspring of Joseph and Elvira) felt for Bellevue, and the tales they told about it, demonstrate that it was an unusually happy place for the eleven children—all of whom lived to maturity except one little boy (Edwin Holt), who died of a contagious disease at about two years of age.

The eleven children of Joseph and Elvira Holt Erwin were: Mary Louise; Elizabeth Matilda; Margaret Locke; Corinna Morehead; William Allen; Adelaide Simianna; James Locke; Jesse Harper; Edwin Holt; Claudia Josephine; and my father, Joseph Ernest, who was born on Christmas Eve, 1867, two years after the Civil War.

It was not until the two eldest children, Mary Louise and Elizabeth Matilda, had been sent off to boarding school at Saint Mary's Episcopal Female Academy at Raleigh, North Carolina, that the first frightening signs of the approaching Civil War began to appear—

which caused the family in the house on the hill to become fearful of the catastrophe and tragedy it would have to face in the dark days that lay ahead.

## Chapter Five

*The Civil War (1861-1865) — Bloody Kirk and the Mountain Desperadoes — The Home Guards — The "Lion Hearted Host"*

5.

Joseph J. Erwin (1811-1879), like his father James Erwin, was born to a life of ease and plenty at Bellevue Plantation about four miles from the village of Morganton, North Carolina. William W. Erwin, the son of the elder of the two brothers to pioneer into the area, had sixteen children, and Alexander Erwin, the younger brother, had five children by his first wife and eight more by his second. Thus, neither brother was slow in increasing the population of the piedmont area.

By nature, Joseph J. Erwin was an intellectual and a scholar and he was sent to Washington College in Virginia (now Washington and Lee), where he "graduated with high honors." He also obtained a law degree but he never practiced law, preferring to live the life of a planter.

According to published records and statements made by those who knew him, he was a very handsome man, and to these records and statements, his portrait gives credence. He was six feet and two and a half inches tall and is described as having "a strong, well proportioned figure, which was much admired." I was told by persons who knew him that he had a "courtly manner and was quick and graceful in his movements." The relatives who told me this also said he had a "straight, well-shaped nose, fair skin and dark eyes and hair."

He was deeply religious and I have often heard it said that "he was a Christian who practiced his religion." His honesty and integrity are traits that were often mentioned by those who spoke of him and he was known as an affectionate and sympathetic husband and father, much respected and loved by his wife and children.

When I was a child, I often heard his daughters, who were my aunts, speak of him in the old-fashioned way as "my saintly father," or "my father who was among the Lord's elect" or in other terms of reverence and endearment. Although reared in the Presbyterian faith, he joined Grace Episcopal Church in Morganton after he married Elvira Jane Holt, an Episcopalian, and he served there as Senior Warden and vestryman for many years.

Elvira was the daughter of Dr. William Rainey Holt, who was a wealthy man and had a handsome home called The Homestead (still standing in 1996) in Lexington, North Carolina, where he lived in the winter months. He had a second home on a two thousand acre plantation near Lexington that was called Linwood, where he spent the summer months. He owned a famous racing horse called Medley, which he raced in Kentucky and other places, often winning large purses. He also owned a large herd of Devon cattle, imported from England, which was considered to be the finest breed of cattle in that day.

His first wife, Elvira's mother, was Mary Gizeal Allen. She died when Elvira was young, but Dr. Holt saw to it that his daughter was well educated. When Elvira married Joseph J. Erwin of Bellevue, she had an elaborate wedding and reception, which was attended by a large crowd of relatives and friends and many prominent persons from different parts of the state. Elvira was of medium height, had fair skin and dark eyes and hair, and she and Joseph were said to make "a handsome pair."

Her wedding dress was made of white silk with an overdress of heavy white lace, both imported from Paris, and her slippers were of white silk with white silk rosettes on the toes. The wedding dress cost fifty dollars in gold, which was quite a large sum for that day, and it was made by a famous modiste in New York City. Since the mails were unreliable, Dr. Holt, fearing the dress would not reach Lexington in time for the wedding, had a courier on horseback to fetch it from New York to his home. Elvira was gifted in literature and.art and played the piano skillfully; and Joseph gave her a handsome piano when they were married.

When I was a child, I was told the piano was made in England, but the large box in which it was delivered to Bellevue is still there in the cellar and has "Baltimore" printed on it; so, perhaps it was shipped from England, sold at Baltimore and then sent to Charleston by ship, after which it was carried to Bellevue by wagon—which would have been a shorter, easier trip than being brought overland from Baltimore.

After the death of Elvira's mother, Dr. Holt married again, this time to a lady who did not show affection to the children by his first wife. Elvira did not find life pleasant with her stepmother; nor did her sister, Mary, and her brother, John. When John was twelve years old, he ran away from home because of his stepmother's unkindness, and after some time he was found working as a water boy on the railroad.

## Chapter Five

On her wedding day, Elvira was hurt and embarrassed by her stepmother's lack of sympathy and kindness as she was preparing to leave on her wedding trip. The carriage already stood at the door with the coachman waiting in his place on the box (which the coachman's high seat in front of a carriage was called in that day), when she missed Jane, the young black maid who was her body servant and with whom she had grown up. She and Jane were devoted to each other and, since Elvira was small when her mother died, she depended upon Jane as though they were sisters. They were continually together and always slept in the same room, but, as she looked about in the crowd for the young woman, she found that Jane was nowhere in sight.

When she asked for Jane, her stepmother replied, "Oh, I have decided to keep her here and have chosen a different maid to go with you."

This was a real blow to Elvira, for she had counted on having Jane with her always, and she wanted Jane to help her start her life in her new faraway home. Although greatly disappointed, Elvira did not want to cause friction with so many wedding guests looking on and upon such a joyous occasion, so she made no protest as the black maid, who was not as smart and dependable as Jane, and whom Elvira did not particularly like, came to join her, already dressed for travel.

It was said that when the stepmother had daughters of her own, she gave them the jewelry that had belonged to Elvira's mother, but Elvira, who I was told, had a loving and forgiving heart, forgave this unkindness. Many years later, after the stepmother had undergone sorrows of her own, Elvira had her to visit at Bellevue, along with her daughters, of whom Elvira became fond. She was especially devoted to her stepsister Claudia, for whom she named one of her own daughters.

Elvira was gregarious, outgoing, and enjoyed entertaining for her children at Bellevue. My father, her youngest child, told me that she often said to her children, "Invite your friends to come in and we'll have a frolic."

In those days a dancing party was often called a frolic, and the young people danced and made merry in the big square parlor in the home on the hill, while Elvira played the piano. Thus the piano Joseph had given Elvira proved to be a great pleasure to the whole family as the years passed. She also enjoyed gathering her children about her and having them sing with her as she played on the big old-fashioned flat-topped instrument. It had keys of ivory and places on each side of the keyboard that were covered with dark red velvet to hold lamps or candles. The piano stool was also covered with dark red velvet.

Since my father, aunts, and uncles, who were Elvira's children, spoke so often of the happy days at Bellevue, I was pleased to be able to read a portion of a diary kept by a teacher, a Miss Gordon, who came from the eastern part of the state to tutor the children at Bellevue before they were old enough to be sent away to boarding school.

On a stormy night not long after her arrival she wrote, "How fortunate I am to be with this kind and gracious family. Colonel Erwin and his wife are so unfailingly kind and interested in my welfare, showing me every attention.

"This evening Mary Louise, who is eight, and Matilda, who is six, and even little Margaret, who is only four, said their pieces in the parlor for their parents and all did quite prettily. Both parents are fond of Shakespeare; so after the little girls had been sent off to bed, I read Shakespeare to them for several hours. It was a bad rainy night, but what a happy time we had beside the parlor fire while the rain pelted against the window panes. Now I am upstairs by my own fire in my comfortable room . . . and so to bed."

After the two oldest girls were sent off to boarding school, a close friend of Joseph Erwin came out from Morganton to pay a call at Bellevue on a pleasant afternoon. As he was going down the front steps to leave, he paused and said, as though it were an afterthought, "By the way, Colonel Erwin, I feel sure you won't mind going security for me on my note."

"Going security" was a common practice between friends of that day, the lender of the money feeling certain that his friend, whom he trusted, was an honest man and would pay back the money at the first possible chance. In fact, he was "honor bound" to do so; for he, too, signed the note. The friend, however, never repaid what he had borrowed (which was a large sum), although he was considered to be one of the wealthiest and most trusted men in the village, and this transaction brought a heavy burden to Joseph Erwin and contributed to his financial ruin.

He had suddenly become poor, like others in the South who had once been wealthy, and he had the care and support of a large family and the operation of a big estate upon him. He believed that after the war, when times grew easier and money was not so scarce, his once trusted friend would pay back what he had borrowed, but he

## Chapter Five

never did.

Instead, he built a new home, which was one of the handsomest in the village. When passing by it as a child, I sometimes thought of how dishonest this man had been, and what financial distress he had caused my grandfather. I also marveled that he had remained highly respected by the citizens, but I decided that perhaps they never learned of his dishonesty. Incidentally, I was told that Joseph Erwin, my grandfather, said on several occasions, "my word is my bond," and that he stuck to this pronouncement all of his life, for he was a very honest man.

While Mary Louise and Matilda were students at Saint Mary's they enjoyed the many social events to which they were invited, especially those at the Governor's Mansion, for Governor Vance was a close friend of their father and he had often visited at Bellevue during their childhood years. Most Southerners thought that the Civil War would not last long, but as the fighting continued and grew worse, the social life in Raleigh diminished.

Sometimes the students at Saint Mary's were allowed to go to the State Capitol when regiments of North Carolina troops gathered there to receive the governor's blessing before marching off to battle, for this was considered to be an important occasion. At times they also saw both Union and Southern troops marching past in the dusty road in front of the school. The Union troops were well dressed and marched briskly, with bands playing and flags flying, but the Southern troops looked increasingly worn and ragged, some of them even being barefoot, or with their feet tied up in carpet scraps.

When the war began, Joseph Erwin was over fifty years old and in poor health. Being too old for military service, he joined the Home Guards which were organized in Morganton, as well as in other villages of the piedmont region and the mountains. The Home Guards were made up of men too old or sickly for fighting, boys who were too young, and soldiers who had been sent home because of wounds or loss of limbs. They were organized to protect the women, children, and aging relatives of the men who had gone off to join the Southern army, but they found that at home they had to face a foe more frightening than the Yankee troops.

These were the gangs of ruffians—lawless and brutal men from various states who had gone into hiding in the mountains of North Carolina and Tennessee to avoid having to fight in either army. Living like savages in crude shelters they had thrown together deep in the forests, or in hollows, ravines, and caves in the mountains, they gathered in groups and preyed upon the unprotected homes.

Plundering and burning houses and sometimes killing the inhabitants, they lived like wild men and acted and looked the part, letting their hair and beards grow long, so that their appearances terrified any person they chanced to meet. As the war continued, pleas were made to the Governor of North Carolina for men to guard the unprotected homes of the region, but the Confederate army, greatly outnumbered from the start, had not a man to spare.

At times these ruffian raiders, on reaching a home, would call out "the man of the house," often a tottering old grandfather or a boy of ten or twelve years of age, and shoot him down before the eyes of his family before stealing whatever they thought might be of value, destroying furniture, ripping up feather beds, taking away livestock, horses, and mules and carrying off all the food they could find. Sometimes called the raiders, the outliers, the land pirates, the desperadoes and other names that struck terror to every victim's heart, they continued to raid through the mountains and carry out whatever nefarious schemes they had in mind. The most feared of these gangs was led by a mountain man named George Kirk, usually referred to as Bloody Kirk, or Old Bloody, because of his brutality.

During this time of confusion and terror, however, there came a little hopeful news for those left in their homes unprotected. In the farther reaches of the mountains, near the Tennessee line, a group of Cherokee Indian braves was being organized to fight for the South and given military training along with white mountain men. This was an arrangement that was brought about by Colonel William H. Thomas, who was a friend of Jefferson Davis, President of the Confederacy, and who was known for his kindness to and work with the Indians.

Colonel Thomas had been born and reared in the distant mountains of North Carolina and had spent his boyhood close to the Cherokee reservation. In 1836-38 he had even prevented their forced removal to the West in the infamous "Trail of Tears."

Consequently, the Cherokees respected him for his honesty and reliability, and, although he was a white man, following the deaths of their old chiefs, Unaguskee and Junaluska, the Indians made him their chief. He had served them wisely and with kindness, conferring with the United States Government on their behalf whenever necessary. On learning of the cruelty occurring at the unprotected homes in the mountains of North Carolina, Colonel Thomas had entered the Confederate army. Soon other mountain men joined him—men who were handpicked for their intelligence, physical strength, courage and bravery—along with Indian braves of the same caliber.

Colonel Thomas organized eight companies of white men and two companies of Indians, so that he soon had 1,700 men, including officers. These men were noted for being physically fit, vigorous, strong, and so courageous that they were called the "Lion Hearted Host"—a name they earned early in the war. Within the ranks of the companies of Indian braves was a young chieftain who became known for his tall stature, magnificent build, strength, and courage. His name was Astooga Stoga, and tales of his prowess and handsome appearance were soon spread throughout the western area of North Carolina.

While the Indians were superior fighters and quick learners of military tactics, they refused to wear uniforms. They carried and became skilled in the use of guns, but they would go into battle only in their usual fashion, their faces and naked bodies painted with war paint and their heads adorned with feathers, according to rank. They wore loin cloths and beaded moccasins and carried hunting knives and tomahawks in their belts. One description of them in battle array reads, "they were painted and feathered off in proper fashion for the battle."

The overall name for the ten companies (white and Indian) was Thomas' Legion of Indians and Highlanders. They became quickly known for their exploits in the mountains near the Tennessee line because they had to be rushed into combat in a number of strategic skirmishes and fights, many of which were caused by Union troops stationed at Knoxville, Tennessee (where the Union Army had established headquarters). Thus, they were never sent into the lower reaches of the mountains to take care of the unprotected homes, for which duty they had been organized, because they were so greatly needed elsewhere.

Unfortunately, in 1862 about a year after the Civil War began, Astooga Stoga was killed and the Indians, forgetting the white man's way of warfare, threw aside their guns, instinctively grabbed their tomahawks, and scalped a number of the enemy before they could be stopped. The mettle of these Indian fighters was well demonstrated during the many fights and skirmishes in which they took part and it was known that they would continue to fight well into the night if they thought it necessary—so long as they could see by the light of the moon.

Thomas' Legion of Indians and Highlanders had its headquarters at Qualla Town on the Cherokee reservation and, by a turn of fate, it was Thomas' Legion, "The Lion Hearted Host," that surrendered last of all the North Carolina troops. Lee surrendered on April 9, 1865 and Johnston surrendered the other portion of the Confederate Army under his charge shortly afterwards, but, due to the scarcity of roads in the mountains and the lack of telegraph facilities, the news that the war had ended did not reach "The Lion Hearted Host" on time. Consequently, it was not until about a month later, in May of 1865, that it finally received word of the surrender while it was fighting near Waynesville, North Carolina.

Bloody Kirk, like a number of mountain men, had sided with the North, and had begun his career by piloting escaped Union prisoners from the Confederate prison at Salisbury, about eighty miles east of Morganton, over the mountains to Union headquarters in Tennessee.

There was little actual fighting in the piedmont area of North Carolina between the Union and Confederate armies during the Civil War, because the lack of roads and the dense forests and rugged terrain of the mountains made the region unsuitable for the marching and maneuvering of troops. As time passed, the mountain raiders, who had no opposition from Thomas' Legion or from either army, grew bolder and in the early fall of 1864 they even penetrated as far east as the Catawba Valley and into the Quaker Meadows area just across the river from Morganton.

Colonel Joseph J. Erwin was away from home with the Home Guards when Bloody Kirk and his men came to Bellevue. It was a black boy, a slave on the place, who was returning from the mill on the plantation, riding a horse and carrying a sack of meal, who first saw the ruffians coming at a fast gallop, followed by a cloud of dust in the avenue that led from the public road.

At once he set up the cry of "Yankee's comin'! Yankee's comin'!", threw down the sack of meal and galloped wildly to the house, where instant pandemonium broke out.

Elvira Erwin went quickly to the front porch and stood awaiting the men at the top of the steps, the terrified children and house servants huddling about her. The raiders jumped their horses over the white picket fence surrounding the front and side lawns and tossed their bridle reins over the low hanging boughs of the large hemlock tree that stood near the front gate. Then they strode up the lawn and demanded to be given whiskey.

Elvira had been told that was the first thing for which they asked, but one of my aunts, who was present at the time, told me that there was no whiskey on the place because "drinking whiskey was against the principles of Mother and Pa."

She also said, "We children were taught that whiskey made a good medicine at times but was a poor beverage."

Every year Elvira had a small amount of wine made from the grapes grown on the place, but except for a little served on holidays such as Thanksgiving and Christmas, it was kept for medicinal purposes only. That year she had the wine made as usual and, in making it, had used the last of the sugar she possessed. Sugar was very hard to get in the South in those days; so she had hidden the wine carefully and bottled the dregs, which were placed in the wine cellar under the house, in case Bloody Kirk and his men should visit Bellevue.

"I have no whiskey, gentlemen," she said. "Only a little grape wine." She turned to a young serving maid, saying "Please show the gentlemen to the wine cellar."

The men grabbed the bottles of dregs and began drinking, but they quickly spat out the bitter liquid, cursing and saying it was the worst wine they had ever tasted. They ransacked the house, going through every room and taking what they wanted, but they did not find the bundle wrapped in a sheet that had been pushed up the parlor chimney.

It contained some jewelry; Elvira's wedding dress and slippers; Joseph's wedding suit and brocaded wedding vest; and a few other garments that were still wearable after several years of war during which new clothing could not be obtained. With the bundle in the parlor chimney, no fire could be made in that room the last year of the war, while it remained in hiding. Nor did Bloody Kirk's men find the family silver, which had been hidden under the attic floor.

The servants refused to let the ruffians know about the silver—until a small black boy was terrified by a raider, who said he would run his bayonet through him if he did not tell—and, on learning where it was, the men tramped up the attic stairs, ripped up boards from the floor and ran their swords and bayonets beneath them, but to no avail.

They also failed to find a handsome gold watch belonging to Joseph Erwin, that he had placed upon the jutting cornice above the front door when he first rode off to join the Home Guards, saying as he did so, that if he were killed, he wanted the watch to be given to his eldest son, William Allen Erwin, who was then about nine years old. Also, fearing the men would steal his horses, mules and other livestock, Joseph had pens built for them up in the woods near the creek, but Bloody Kirk found and took most of them.

Amusing events sometimes occur during desperate times, and there was one that gave the family a good laugh after Bloody Kirk's departure. "Aunt Dicie," the beloved old black cook at Bellevue, was fond of fried chicken; and feeling certain the raiders would steal the chickens, she had jerked handfuls of feathers from the poor fowls, which gave them a sickly, unappetizing look, and the raiders left them alone.

My aunts said they could not help laughing when they heard one of the men say, "Them chickens are shedding so bad they must be ailin'. We'd best to leave 'em alone."

Because of this scheme Aunt Dicie had hit upon, the chickens, along with the eggs they produced, became major staples in the family diet at Bellevue when food was scarce during the last years of the Civil War and afterward. The family had feared Bloody Kirk would burn down the house, as he had other homes, but they learned later that he was in a hurry because he wanted to destroy some supplies for the Confederate Army that were stored in boxcars at "the head of the road"—the place where the railroad to the western part of the state ended about six miles east of Morganton.

The boxcars had been left there for an engine to carry them to the battlefront, and, on reaching them, Bloody Kirk stole what he wanted, burned the cars and then dashed on to Camp Vance a short distance away, where boys too young for military service were being trained for battle because of the South's desperate need for troops.

He forced the boys to mount behind his men on their horses, to serve as shields, in case the Home Guards should follow them. This the Home Guards did, but they were forced to hold their fire, for fear of killing the boys. The raiders escaped with the boys to Union headquarters in Tennessee by taking a precipitous route over the mountains that was called the Winding Stairs, and the boys were then sent to prison in Arkansas.

The family at Bellevue, on learning that the Union General Kilpatrick was advancing with his army on Lexington, North Carolina, where Elvira's father, Dr. William Rainey Holt, and his second wife and their children lived, became apprehensive as to what might happen. It turned out, however, that like the Bellevue cook, Aunt Dicie, Mrs. Holt had thought of a ruse to outwit the Yankees. Dr. Holt was not at home at the time, having gone to Linwood, his plantation, to try to save what he could, "as he had fine cattle and much cotton on hand," and his wife feared that Kilpatrick might take over their home in Lexington as his headquarters, since it was considered to be the finest in town.

With this in mind, she sent Jerry, her butler, to meet the general at the edge of town to invite him to make her home his headquarters. The surprised General Kilpatrick accepted her invitation and, although the American flag was hung at her front gate, and the sentinels patrolling across her front lawn wore a path through the grass, her home was not molested, whereas many other homes were plundered and citizens were abused.

Fearful for the safety of her young lady daughters, she kept two upstairs bedrooms for the family's use and had the doors of these rooms fitted with strong locks and iron brackets, across which a thick plank could be placed as an extra security measure. She made a point of being friendly with the Union officers and eating meals with them, but her daughters, who did not approve of her actions, sulked upstairs and their meals had to be sent up to them.

Thenie and Mandy, two upstairs maids, told the girls that one of the officers had in his room a large trunk filled with beautiful clothes for ladies and some silver that he said he had taken from a lady in South Carolina.

General Kilpatrick had with him many fine horses he had captured in the South and he offered to give Mrs. Holt a pair for her carriage. Kas, her coachman, begged her to accept them but she would not, knowing they had been taken from a Southern family. Although sugar and coffee could not be obtained in the South at that time, General Kilpatrick had plenty of each and furnished Mrs. Holt with both of these desired staples. The sugar was in blocks that weighed twenty-five pounds each and when he left, he gave her several—one of which she saved to make the wedding cakes for her eldest daughter.

His most valued gift, however, was some pieces of gold, which she said, "were about all they had to take them through the poverty stricken days ahead." He also gave her daughter Amelia a beautiful black pony, which the girl refused to take at first, but later accepted with reluctance.

In the early spring of 1865, as the war dragged on, conditions became so frightening that Elvira and Joseph Erwin decided that their eldest daughters, Mary Louise and Matilda, should not remain at boarding school but should come home to Bellevue, and Joseph Erwin decided to go to fetch them. Taking with him a trusted black body servant, each of them on horseback and well armed, he rode to Raleigh to escort the stagecoach that was to bring his daughters home, hoping to protect it from any troubles it might encounter on the way.

This was a dangerous undertaking because of the "bummers" — Union soldiers who deserted their commands temporarily when it suited them to do so, to prey upon Southern homes along their line of march and to capture vehicles, mules and horses on the highways.

When stealing the vehicles and animals, they took the luggage of the passengers as well, often leaving the travelers stranded far from any sort of help; and if the terrified victims made any protest they were apt to be treated roughly or even killed. Aware of this, the family at the house on the hill was fearful about the safety of Joseph and his man on the trip to Raleigh, and also that of the two girls.

Consequently, the family was filled with anxiety on seeing Joseph depart, not knowing what catastrophe might occur or if the little group would ever return safely to Bellevue.

## Chapter Six

*A Dangerous Stagecoach Ride —*
*When the Yankee Cavalry Came to Morganton —*
*The Surrender, Heartbreak and Poverty —*
*The End of an Era*

### 6.

Through unexpected good fortune, the trip to Raleigh turned out successfully and the group arrived at Bellevue without mishap. Thankful to be safe at home at last, they were nonetheless fearful that Bloody Kirk and his men might return at any moment. There were rumors that he was building a fort at Blowing Rock, which meant he would not have to come all the way over the mountains from Tennessee on a raid but could sweep down into the Catawba Valley and into Morganton in a much shorter time.

Aunt Mary Louise, the older of the two sisters, told me when she was an old lady, "Of course, we were frightened all the more by this, and it put us all in a bustle, trying to hide even more than we had already hidden from the brutal mountain raiders, not knowing what day or hour they would appear."

Soon, however, they heard that a different and equally frightening foe was advancing in their direction. This was the Yankee General Stoneman, who was coming with his cavalry through the mountains on the west.

In March, a few months after they arrived at home, Aunt Mary Lou, who was sixteen at the time, began a diary in which she wrote, "On the 28th of March the people of Burke County were very much excited on receiving intelligence that General Stoneman with five or six thousand men was in the Valley of the Yadkin. He camped there that night at the Yadkin Factory belonging to the Patterson Company, which he burnt on leaving, and instead of attacking Morganton, as we expected, he bent his course toward Wilkesboro."

The Valley of the Yadkin River was about fifteen miles from Bellevue and the Yankee cavalry was moving with unusual swiftness through difficult mountain passes, lighted in night travel by torches held by mountaineers who were sympathetic to the Union. The family in the home on the hill knew it would not be long before they reached Morganton and it was also apparent to them, as to all Southerners, that the South, with its much smaller number of troops, as well as a smaller amount of ammunitions and other supplies necessary to making war, could not hold out much longer and defeat would soon follow.

At the time, however, they were unaware of the fact that Stoneman's orders were not to fight battles but to complete the breaking of Southern morale by destroying its war-making capacity and impoverishing the land itself by living off its produce as he went.

Stopping at Salisbury, he began his "burnt earth policy," for Salisbury, although a small town, was of immense importance to the South. As a Confederate Commissary Headquarters, it dispensed food and supplies to the Confederate army. It had several hospitals for wounded Southern soldiers brought in by train; an extensive passenger car shed, two freight depots, a foundry, a prison, a steam distillery, an arsenal, a large Confederate government building, and a number of ordinance buildings.

All of these Stoneman put to the torch, and the burning buildings, exploding shells and magazines, and the flames that illuminated the skies all night made it appear for miles around that a terrible battle was being fought.

For days after this, women and children, near starvation, searched the smoking ruins for food; and Elvira learned that her brother, John Holt, was a victim of the destruction. He was a wealthy man and owned what was described as "an extensive private tannery that caught fire from the nearby burning buildings and was destroyed."

As Stoneman and his cavalry continued on toward Morganton, they demolished whatever could be of help to General Lee, in case he should decide to turn southward—especially factories; iron foundries; and railroads, the rails of which were heated to a glowing red and then wrapped around trees so they could never be used again. He also led many slaves away from their homes. Food was already scarce in the South and this brought starvation still closer, since there would soon be few persons left to cultivate the fields.

By now, the family at Bellevue and others living in Morganton and its environs were so alarmed, that Colonel Thomas Walton, head of the little group of Home Guards, stationed his men on the north side of the village where they waited for the Yankee cavalry to appear. A brief skirmish took place at that point and the children at Bellevue were terrified by the noises of battle and the cannon ball that sailed over the Catawba River and ploughed across the front lawn at Bellevue not far from the house.

Entering Morganton, Stoneman's cavalry drove the little band of Home Guards before it and found the streets empty and deserted, with all windows shuttered and all doors locked. They broke into

## Chapter Six

every home, barn, and smokehouse, stripping the village of foodstuffs and taking whatever they wanted. Some of them went into the surrounding areas, ransacking homes in the valley and taking away horses, mules and other livestock, but my aunts told me, "they did not find much to steal at Bellevue, because Bloody Kirk had already stolen whatever he desired and stripped the place bare." They found the few horses and mules that Bloody Kirk had left and took them and as much foodstuffs as they could find, leaving the family with little to eat; and, in order to discomfort it still further, they ripped up featherbeds and destroyed furniture and furnishings in the home.

When the Yankee soldiers told Aunt Mary Lou that Lee had surrendered (on April 9, 1865) she wrote in her diary that she would not believe it until she "heard it from the lips of our own brave soldiers in the Confederacy." When Abraham Lincoln was killed not long after this, she wrote that she could not understand why "the daring Booth could commit such an act, but its cause must have been patriotic, as he must have known that he would be killed as a result."

After all the horses and mules were stolen, the family at Bellevue had no way to go to the village to find out what was happening there or elsewhere. They could not walk to town because the road to Morganton passed through the river ford, and horses or mules were needed to cross through the water.

However, after several weeks without news, Mary Lou and Matilda decided upon a plan of "going to town by the canoe", about which she wrote in her diary. This meant that they walked the mile to the river ford and were rowed across the water in a canoe by a Mr. Fleming who lived near the ford.

They walked the rest of the way to town and spent the night in town with their cousin, Corinna Morehead Avery. The lady tutor at Bellevue and their younger brother, William, walked with them to the river and returned to meet them there when they came home. It is interesting to note that it was thought to be safe for young girls to go about in this manner so soon after the war ended. However, I was told that, for several months following the end of the hostilities and before the North had taken over, the Southern people seemed to be stunned and there was "a strange, mysterious calm, like that which follows a devastating storm."

As President Jefferson Davis fled southward, he paused at Charlotte, North Carolina, and the last full meeting of the Confederate Cabinet was held there at the home of William F. Phifer, who was a relative of Colonel Joseph Erwin. Members of the Erwin family of Bellevue had often visited there, and in my youth the Phifer home was still standing and was a large, handsome house built of brick that stood on a spacious lot facing North Tryon Street a few blocks from the center of town.

As General Sherman turned northward at the end of the war, after burning a swath fifty miles wide from Atlanta to the sea, he destroyed most of Charleston, wrecked Columbia, South Carolina and continued on toward Raleigh, the capital of North Carolina. Since North Carolina had seen less actual fighting than most of the other Confederate states, it was hoped that Sherman would be more lenient towards it. However, the people feared what he might do to Raleigh and its handsome Capitol Building, which strongly resembled certain Greek temples, particularly the Temple of the Goddess Minerva.

Because of this, a hurried plan was made to send Governor Zebulon Vance to meet Sherman and plead for leniency. However, Vance had been a Confederate soldier and it was feared this might count against him. A second choice for this endeavor was Governor William A. Graham, who had served as a United States Senator for many years as well as Secretary of the United States Navy in the cabinet of President Fillmore. Graham was an elderly man and in failing health at the time, but he was still highly respected and trusted by the people of the state and he agreed to go. With a few other prominent men, he went by train from Greensboro to Raleigh under a flag of truce and met Sherman in his tent near Raleigh, where the group talked all night—the result being that Raleigh was left in peace.

General Johnston surrendered the last of the Confederate troops, which were under his command, a short time after this at Durham Station about thirty miles west of Raleigh and the war was over—except for the battle that was fought in the North Carolina mountains near Waynesville where news of the surrender had not reached Thomas' Legion of Indians and Highlanders, the famous "Lion Hearted Host."

When Colonel Joseph J. Erwin of Bellevue died of pneumonia on November 20, 1879, my father (the youngest of the ten living children) was only eleven years old and Elvira was left without a loving and protective husband to help her run the plantation. At the time of Joseph's death, it was the custom to write the death message in black ink on white, black-bordered paper. The message indicat-

## Chapter Six

ed that the death had taken place and gave the hour and day of the funeral and burial. A veil of sheer black crepe was placed over the notice, tied with a black grosgrain ribbon; and, if a delicate white bud or flower could be had at the time, it was knotted into the ribbon.

The notice was placed on a silver tray and a black manservant, dressed in black with a black crepe mourning band about his sleeve, carried the tray to relatives and friends who lived here and there in the valley and in town. The recipient of the notice lifted the veil, read the message and replaced the veil—after which it was carried to the next person on the list.

When Colonel Samuel McDowell Tate of Morganton read the notice, he took a piece of paper from his pocket and wrote upon it some words from the Bible, saying that when he thought of Colonel Joseph J. Erwin, the words he had written came at once into his mind. He said that, if Colonel Erwin's widow thought well of it, he thought they would make a suitable epitaph for her husband's gravestone. Elvira agreed with him and these words can be seen today on the white marble shaft that marks his grave in the little churchyard at Grace Episcopal Church in Morganton. They are:

> Mark the perfect man,
> And behold the upright;
> For the end of that man is peace.
> (Psalm 37-37)

Numerous memorials and statements about Colonel Joseph J. Erwin were printed in newspapers and periodicals at the time of his death, and I have included a few that may throw additional light upon the personality and character of the man.

One journalist wrote, "Nothing written about Colonel Erwin would be complete which omitted reference to his Christian character, the key to the whole machinery of the man."

Another states:

> "Colonel Erwin was a model of the old time Southern planter as developed under the mild patriarchal form of slavery existing in Virginia and upper North Carolina. A sketch of the habits, manners, ways of thought and political and religious inclinations of such a man would be of value to future generations."

In another memorial we read:

"It was not in public life that Colonel Erwin delighted, although he served as Justice of the Court of Pleas and Quarter Sessions and Clerk of the County Court, following his father, James Erwin, and his grandfather, Alexander Erwin, in those offices, and was also for several times, a member of the North Carolina State Legislature. His pleasure was, rather, to do good than to appear great. An ample purse, a noble county seat, and the most cultured surroundings enabled him to dispense at his home an old-fashioned Southern hospitality until the defeat and impoverishment of the South after the Civil War; and after that, sadly hurt in purse and heart, advanced in years and having on him the care of a large family, he faced the future with courage and fortitude."

Another writer asks:

"Who has enjoyed the delightful welcome of Colonel Erwin's roof can forget his old time courtesy, the merry twinkle of his fine dark eye when an apt word of humor was thrown into the dialogue, his companiable freedom with the young members of his household, the charity of his criticism and his unspeakable scorn of any mean action?"

As for his appearance, another article states, "In his youth he must have been a most handsome man. He was tall and shapely, possessed of an active well knit frame and a strong constitution, along with a quickness of movement and grace that he had inherited from his father, James Erwin."

Governor Zebulon Vance, who knew him well and often visited at his home, wrote of him, "In private life he was looked upon as an Exemplar of all that is good in the being of a man. He was the soul of integrity and had as nice a sense of honor as any Paladin of Romance."

Many years after his death a well-known journalist wrote: "Joseph J. Erwin is still held up in Burke County as a man who filled a long life so worthily that when he died no man found a sign of error in all his years but good deeds and righteousness and lov-

# Chapter Six

ableness."

After Joseph's death, Elvira was forced to take over the management of the plantation and it became apparent in time that she had business ability that she had not known she possessed. In fact, she was to become an excellent business woman, and under her management the plantation would begin to yield again. Although her many activities relative to running the place kept her busy, she never neglected her morning devotions, for, like her husband, she was deeply religious. She rose from bed early and had her morning cup of coffee in her bedroom. Following this, she said her prayers and read her Prayer Book and Bible. She went to breakfast and then began her business of the day.

In time, Elvira Erwin's sons and daughters married and moved away to homes of their own in other places—except her two eldest daughters, Mary Lou and Matilda, who never married—and my father, who, after his marriage, settled in the nearby village of Morganton.

As Elvira grew older, she did not lose interest in people. She continued to invite her friends to visit her at Bellevue and also enjoyed visiting them. On one of her wedding anniversaries her two eldest daughters gave her a "spend-the-day-party" and among the guests were some elderly ladies who had been bridesmaids in her wedding.

They wore the gold heart-shaped pins pierced by a gold arrow that she had given them on her wedding day, and I was told that as they sat together in the parlor, chatting and reminiscing about the past, their eyes often filled with tears over memories both happy and sad.

Later Aunt Matilda reported that, "The party was a great success. They laughed and cried all day, and had a wonderful time."

Elvira remained mentally alert until her death. Her religion continued to be the mainstay of her life, and a number of memorials were published in major newspapers of the state after her death that may help to add more information about her, a few of which I include.

One in the *News and Observer* of Raleigh reads:

"Mrs. Erwin was born in Lexington, North Carolina on November 12, 1824 and was the daughter of Dr. William Rainey

Holt. In 1847 she married Colonel Joseph J. Erwin of Bellevue in Burke County and shortly after their marriage they moved to Rutherford County and lived on Broad River for several years, where her husband managed the gold mining business of his father. After the death of Colonel James Erwin, they moved to Bellevue and Mrs. Erwin lived there continuously until her death. Her husband's ancestry, like her own, was distinguished. Bellevue, a magnificent property situated on the banks of Upper Creek and the Catawba River, had been granted by the Earl of Granville to Colonel Alexander Erwin, although the Erwins had lived on the estate prior to that time, and for a century, Alexander, James and Joseph Erwin were prominent men, highly esteemed in public and private life."

One memorial article states:

"Mrs. Erwin kept her house in order, not only in a social and domestic way but in a business way. As a manager of property interest of whatever kind, she had few equals even among men. She was a Christian who made daily use of her religion and it was the mainstay of her life. As a friend she was faithful to the utmost and she weighted all human relationships with love."

Another memorial states:

"Mrs. Erwin lived tenderly close to her children and they gave her rich reward throughout the years. Though as the years passed they left her in a measure, her household always held together and she kept love rife wherever she was. The beauty of early relationships she sustained to a wonderful degree."

And still another says:

"Morganton, North Carolina
Special to The Charlotte Observer, August 24, 1903

"After a long illness Mrs. Elvira Jane Erwin, widow of the late Joseph J. Erwin of Burke County, died yesterday afternoon at four o'clock at Bellevue, her home three and a half miles north of this city.

"Death came peacefully. There was no wasting away of faculties. Ten children were at the bedside; and the mother fervently blessed each in turn and turned happily away from a long and beautiful life.

"Burke County, famed for its colonial houses, has yet marked the decadence of such establishments. The time had come at length when Bellevue, alone, contained a mistress who had learned to rule in the ante-bellum days, and in holding the past as a sacred thing, had kept alive the best living and traditions of the Old South. And now, since yesterday, the voice of the Old South is dead even at Bellevue.

"The funeral services, which were conducted at Grace Episcopal Church at 4 o'clock by the rector, Rev. Mr. Hughson, were simple but impressive. After the usual funeral exercises and the singing of hymns, "Asleep in Jesus" and "Lead, Kindly Light", sympathetic friends gathered at the graveside in the old churchyard and watched the interment by the side of her husband. The pallbearers were: Honorary: Capt. George Phifer Erwin, Judge A.C. Avery, Dr. J. L. Laxton, Dr. P. L. Murphy, I.I. Davies and Dr. James Anderson. Active: Messrs. Frank P. Tate, Sterling R. Collett, Charles Edmonson, Manley McDowell, S.J. Ervin, A.C. Avery Jr. and I. E. Avery.

"A number of relatives and friends from a distance attended the funeral. Relatives surviving Mrs. Erwin are a sister, Mrs. Anderson Ellis and three half-sisters: Mrs. D.C. Pearson of Morganton, Mrs. William E. Holt of Charlotte; and Mrs. C.A. Hunt of Lexington.

"Many friends laid a wealth of flowers on the new-made grave. I was struck by the personnel of the gathering. All classes were represented; I noticed especially those who were representatives of the Old South: the elder gray-haired men and the aged Negroes.

"Children whose sires had ruled other colonial homes were there. Here was represented Creekside by Col. Thomas Walton; there Swan Ponds by Judge Avery; Quaker Meadows by Manley McDowell; Magnolia by Mrs. George Phifer, daughter of Clarke Moulton Avery; Sleepy Hollow by James, John and Frank McDowell; Willow Hill by Mrs. S.R. Collett; Cherry Field by Mrs. M.R. Collett; Happy Valley by members of the Perkins family; and Brookwood by the sons of William Walton."

"All men stood with uncovered heads to do respect and honor to the mistress of Bellevue.

"So passed an admired and greatly respected lady of the Old South."


An era marked by both prosperity and poverty had gone with the turning of the century and what lay ahead of good or ill for the South no one could foretell.

# PART TWO
(1900-1920)

## PART TWO
### (1752-1900)
*Ladies and Gentlemen of The Old School — Horses and Mules— Surreys and Carryalls — Covered Wagons and Mountainfolk — Bucephalus — Miss Sue — Polly Malindy — Old Man Ballew — Confederate Memorial Day — Beautiful Aunt Claudia — The Witch Lady — The Wooden Leg*

### 1.

After I had finished writing Part One of these sketches I felt I had fulfilled my promise to my young relatives to put on paper the tales of long ago for which they had asked, but they begged me to continue.

"Don't stop," they urged. "Tell us about the time that came later — when you were a child. Was it very different from today?"

Was it different from today?

It was so different that I did not even feel able to describe it adequately.

The small town which that earlier village had become has changed so much from what it was when I was a child that it sometimes seems as though it never actually existed.

Still, the more I think about it, the more vividly it comes back to me across the years. In fact, I find that I can remember almost verbatim brief conversations that took place when I was quite young, while with many longer ones I am still aware of the intent of the speakers.

What I probably remember best of all was that it was a time when good manners were important. Girls were taught to be ladies and boys to be gentlemen, and both sexes were taught to be modestly and neatly dressed. It was a time before women wore pants and shorts in public and before men wore long flowing hair, earrings and necklaces.

Gentlemen made a point of showing respect to ladies, and they bowed and lifted their hats to ladies of their acquaintance whom they met upon the street. If a lady paused and engaged them in conversation they stood respectfully with their hats off until she had finished the conversation and had gone upon her way.

They opened doors for ladies, who passed through ahead of them, and helped ladies to mount up into or get down out of carriages, buggies and other horse drawn vehicles that were used for transportation in those days.

If a lady entered a room in which a gentleman was sitting he arose at once and remained standing until she was seated or left the room. Most important of all, ladies and gentlemen were expected to have high morals. Illegitimacy was rare and never spoken of in "polite society," and couples got married before living together.

We never locked our doors and windows by day or night, simply because there appeared to be no reason for doing so. Nor was anyone afraid to walk about the streets of the little town after dark for fear of being mugged, shot at or killed, as they might be in certain towns and cities of today. However, the South was not without heavy burdens at the time. It was still in many ways a wreckage of the Civil War and the Reconstruction Period that followed it, and it was struggling to make the change from an agricultural to a manufacturing region, an almost impossible task.

Although the Civil War had put an end to the prosperous antebellum days, the inhabitants of the village did not forget that it had once enjoyed the distinction of being the only town in the state that had been "born a court town," having been established to be the legal center of the newly formed county of Burke, and that for many years the State Supreme Court left the capital at Raleigh and journeyed there to hold court. Added to this was the prominence it acquired because more gold was mined in the area at a certain time than in any other place in the nation, and because of these unprecedented events, it was sometimes referred to as "The Gem in the Wilderness."

Many of the members of the gentry were proud of the fact that they were related by blood to some of the most prominent families in North Carolina and adjoining states and that the area was known for the number of large, fine old homes in the town and on the plantations in the valley. Nor was this all. As time passed, the area enjoyed the reputation of being "the center of refinement and culture" in western North Carolina—in spite of the fact that few of the streets in town were paved and horses and mules continued to offer its only real means of transportation until after the turn of the century.

What I saw mostly upon its unpaved, quiet and tree shaded streets in my early childhood were buggies, surreys and carryalls. The latter two were two-seaters with fringed canopies on top, the main difference between them being that the surrey required two horses while the carryall needed only one. The old-fashioned closed carriage, the Victoria (named for Queen Victoria of England and her favorite mode of transportation), the cabriolet and other vehicles had gone out of style, but there were wagons and carts used for hauling, which were usually drawn by mules.

An intriguing vehicle that I saw from time to time was an old-fashioned covered wagon belonging to some mountaineer who had come down from one of the nearer mountains to view the "city sights" and to enjoy a brief holiday away from home. When the mountainfolk were interested in litigation at the Courthouse, a number of these wagons appeared, and the men, women and children who rode in them were a picturesque lot; they looked as though they had somehow stepped from between the pages of a book. The women wore sunbonnets and long, full skirted dresses of calico or gingham. The men wore homespun trousers and often jackets of tanned hide, with hats of woven straw or worn, misshapen felt, and about all of them there was a certain appealing Gypsy-like charm.

The wagons seemed to be always overflowing with children, quilts, bedding, pots, pans, and other paraphernalia needed for a short visit away from home. I noticed that there always hung from the pole that projected from the rear a tin water bucket holding a tin dipper and that under this walked a solemn "hound dog" that had been trained to keep to that place and to pace its steps to the slow turning of the wagon wheels.

At night they camped in the center of town in the vacant lot next to the Courthouse between Green and Sterling Streets, and, since we lived on King Street where the public library now stands, we were close enough to see from our front porch the glow from their campfires against the darkening sky as they set about cooking their evening meals. Then after dark, we enjoyed listening to the strumming of their banjos and the high, sweet keening of their fiddles calling through the night as they enjoyed a social interval before going to bed in their wagons.

In those days there were certain gentlemen who still enjoyed going about on horseback at times, and my father was one of them. He rode a large and handsome saddle horse named Bucephalus, after the famous war horse of Alexander the Great, and he was often asked to lead the parades that took place from time to time riding Bucephalus, for the village enjoyed this type of entertainment. He had no military uniform because he had never been the right age to be in a war, so on these occasions he wore a navy blue uniform trimmed with gold buttons and braid with a visored cap to match and a sheathed sword at his hip—the uniform that he had worn when he was on the Governor's staff.

He was a handsome man and a skillful rider, so he and Bucephalus made a much admired sight, in which Bucephalus appeared to take pride. He often danced in time to the music of the hometown band that always marched in the parades, bowing and tossing his head at the clapping of hands as they passed along.

Bucephalus had a stall in our stable next to that of Ginny, an unpredictable mule that belonged to Jim, our butler. Ginny was accorded this privilege because she afforded transportation for Jim and the other servants who rode with him in his cart to Sunday afternoon services at Willow Tree Colored Baptist Church several miles up the river.

There were also a few ladies who continued to go about on horseback in those early days and they came mostly from the old homes on the plantations in the valley. They had ridden horses all their lives, were excellent riders, and they rode sidesaddle, of course; at that time no one dreamed that a lady would ever so far "forget herself" as to straddle a horse. They wore riding skirts so long and voluminous that no glimpse could be caught of an ankle or leg, since it was taboo for a lady to "expose herself."

With them they brought "horse stops," so that they could hitch their horses wherever they wished, on a street or in a driveway at the home of a friend. These "horse stops" were made of polished black iron and were about the size and weight of an old-fashioned clothes pressing iron. They were flat on the bottom and rounded on top with a metal ring that could be attached to a horse's bridle by a long narrow leather strap. They had enough weight when the strap was tugged to convince a horse that it was hitched, although the gadget had only been placed on the ground beside it.

One of the first sidewalks in town to be paved was on the other side of the street in front of our house (the sidewalk on our side was covered with gravel), so it was there that I skated with other children, both girls and boys, of the neighborhood.

Our yard, which was large and not far from the center of town, early became a gathering place for children, and, with the idea of keeping us close to home, my parents had installed on a side lawn a swing, a hammock, a joggling board, a seesaw and a merry-go-round. We climbed trees, of which there were many, jumped rope, hopscotched, and pretended we were tightrope walkers at the circus as we walked the narrow board that ran along near the top of the six foot high plank fence that surrounded the large grassy lot, where Bucephalus and Ginny grazed peacefully together. In the carriage house stood an old but still handsome and well preserved Victoria that, for some unknown reason, had been left there by a relative who had owned the home before my father bought it at the time of his marriage. The Victoria we enjoyed for many years, taking turns playing at being a coachman on the high box seat in front or as passengers, sitting on the tufted black leather seat and the little pull-out seats in the back.

We were taken to the circus, which pitched its big sagging brown tent on Fairground Hill at the edge of town. We also attended the Chautauqua that performed under a tent that was put up on the grounds of the Graded School on Green Street (across from the Courthouse), which appeared to be a suitable place because its programs were of an educational nature. We sat on uncomfortable folding wooden chairs with our feet planted on a carpet of freshly cut wood shavings, our eyes glued to the brightly lit stage upon which Swiss Yodelers yodeled, dancers danced, wearing colorful costumes of different European nations, and simple "family type" plays were presented.

My father liked animals and through the years saw to it that there were always some on the place. Among them were dogs; cats; rabbits; ponies; a squirrel in a cage that cavorted and ran on a spinning barrel of wire; sheep and lambs; a beautiful, long-tailed golden pheasant in an unusually large cage; and even a few goats that afforded much interest and excitement because they liked to butt children who teased or annoyed them.

Since there were no swimming pools, we went to the river to swim or to the creek at Bellevue, my father's old home. There was an unusual place on the creek bank where it curved in a wide arc and the area was covered with white sand as silky and soft as any found on an ocean beach. My father enjoyed taking a group of children there for a swim and a picnic, and the Episcopal Church also held its annual picnic there.

There was no country club and no golf course, and people entertained at receptions, teas, and parties at their homes. Since our house was large and the front hall was wide, as I grew older it became a place for social gatherings and we rolled up the rug and danced to tunes played on a Victrola. When the Duke Power Company built a large and beautiful lake about ten miles from town, many people erected summer cottages around it. Most of the cottages had a large front room in which parties and dancing took place. We also boated on and swam in the lake.

On Sundays, families went to church in a group, as a matter of course. All stores and places of business were closed, and card playing and dancing on Sunday were thought to be inspired by the devil. If young people grew bored or restless, it was suggested to them that going over Sunday school lessons was a profitable way to spend their time, or they could go calling on a friend, particularly one who was ailing. On Sunday afternoons the servants went to the churches to which they belonged and were not expected to do any household chores until Monday morning.

When thinking of meals, I remember our large vegetable garden, which was planted and tended by a short, bow-legged man called Mr. Fisher. He came to town from the country in a large farm wagon hitched to a mule, with which he also plowed the garden. Consequently, we were supplied with plenty of fresh vegetables. The few extra ingredients needed for cooking were bought at the town grocery store on Main Street. There was no meat at the grocery store; it had to be purchased at the meat market. As for chickens, there was a chicken yard and chicken house in every back yard.

Ladies did not go to the grocery store or meat market in those days. Instead, they or their cooks telephoned their orders, which were delivered by boys, both black and white, on bicycles that had baskets on the front of the handlebars. I often felt sorry for these boys because they were pursued by the dogs of every neighborhood into which they ventured. In my mind, I can still see them trying to pedal with one foot and kicking out with the other foot at the dogs that circled them, barking ferociously, while they had to keep the grocery baskets from tipping over and spilling their contents onto the dusty unpaved street.

As we grew older and our more childish games began to pall, we found a new interest that was a little more edifying. We went down to the big brick house at the corner of King and Main Streets two blocks away, and sat in the bushes under the parlor window to listen to Miss Sue Tate, a middle-aged, highly respected maiden lady, practicing on the piano the hymns she planned to play and sing at the Sunday school of the Presbyterian Church.

We did not think Miss Sue's voice was melodious, to say the least, but she played and sang loudly. In fact, she played so loudly that it

## Chapter One

seemed to us that she kept her foot planted on the loud pedal of the piano most of the time. Thus, her voice and the intensified sound caused by the pressure of her foot upon the pedal blended in a peculiar and somewhat menacing manner, so that we never could tell if the ensuing growling sound came from Miss Sue or from the pedal.

Some of the words of the hymns she played were not entirely clear, but we noted that the one she played and sang often had words that sounded like:

> *"Hold the fort, for I am coming!"*
> *Jesus calls us still.*
> *Send the answer back to heaven,*
> *"By Thy Grace we will!"*

Although Miss Sue was religious and the bellwether of the Presbyterian Sunday School, she was known to be quite proud of her family's position in the community and especially of the fact that her father, a respected gentleman who had passed away before I was born, had been an officer in the Confederate army and had fought at Gettysburg, which in that day was enough to make any Southerner proud. Due to these facts, she assumed that she was known by everyone in the village. One story is told that Miss Sue received quite a blow to her pride one day when she bought an article in a store on Main Street and requested that it be charged to her and sent to her home.

The clerk, a rather naive country boy, replied, "But, ma'am, who is you and where do you live?"

Miss Sue, who was short of stature, drew herself up to her full height and demanded, "You mean to tell me you don't know me and don't even know where I live?"

The youth, withering under her sharp and penetrating eye, replied, "No, ma'am, I can't say as how I do."

At this, Miss Sue ordered, "In that case, just cancel my order and I will go to another store where I and the location of my home are known." And, with this termination of the conversation, she sailed out of the store with her head held high.

Because of her standing in the community and her leadership in the Presbyterian Church, we children stood in awe of Miss Sue and were not surprised that a day came when she ascended to the top of one of the nearer mountains, accompanied by a Presbyterian lady friend, and established there a church and a school for the edification and salvation of the mountainfolk — Presbyterian, of course, since she believed this to be the only faith that could ensure a true route to heaven.

There, high upon the mountain peak, she taught, sang and played the piano, her foot clamped continually upon the loud pedal of the piano, I feel sure, while she also kept a sharp eye on the Presbyterians down in the valley—a task that would have been impossible for any lady who was not of Miss Sue's caliber. In fact, we felt that the angels themselves must have watched with approval as she "held the fort" not only on the mountaintop, but down in the valley as well.

Another voice I remember that was entirely different from Miss Sue's, but which still echoes in my ears at times, was that of Polly Malindy, a stalwart but elderly mountain woman, who came to town from time to time to sell her wares, and who was much beloved by all of the children in our neighborhood. Polly Malindy was a giant of a woman, rawboned and muscular and a few inches over six feet in height. Her white hair was bobbed at the same short length all the way around, as though a shallow bowl had been placed upon her head and the hair clipped just under its rim, and throughout the years she wore the same red plaid calico dress that reached to her ankles.

Upon her head, summer and winter, sat a man's straw hat with the tail feathers from many roosters stuck into the hat band. On her feet were man-sized shoes, thick soled and scuffed, and in the winter she also wore a man's brown and faded overcoat over the red plaid calico dress. In an ancient wagon with wheels that creaked mournfully, and behind a big brown mule named Zeke, she rode up and down our street calling out what she had for sale, and the children in the neighborhood ran joyfully to meet her and walked beside her wagon as she rode along, seeming to be delighted by our presence. In the summertime her wagon was filled with apples, peaches, cantaloupes, and grapes (which she called "gripes"), and in winter with short lengths of pine wood for lighting fires (which she called kindlin' wood), galax leaves, holly, mistletoe, and handwoven baskets.

"Kindlin' wood and hand wove baskits!" she would cry in a high pitched nasal voice as she rode along. "Galax leaves—holly berries and mistletoe! Come and git 'em whilst ye may!"

When we thought the people who lived in the homes along our street did not appear with appropriate alacrity to buy her wares, we children, wanting to help the old woman, rang doorbells with such energy that they could be heard jangling throughout the houses.

"Kindlin' wood and hand wove baskits!" we shrieked. "Galax leaves and mistletoe! Come and git 'em whilst ye may!"—which usually brought out cooks and maids with trays, buckets and money in hand, since the ladies on the street wanted to help the old woman, too.

Polly Malindy was illiterate and unread, but she had the bluest eyes I have ever seen, eyes that were quick to soften and grow warm at the sight of a small child, particularly a baby (which she called "a lap child"); and with her there always seemed to come a fresh, clean breeze blowing from the mountains, laden with the scent of balsam and pine and the fleeting fragrance of wild flowers growing in distant upland meadows.

With our help, she could sell her wares with dispatch, so she was soon able to turn her thoughts to a more romantic matter; for, to the amazement of the village, she had fallen in love with the town butcher, a handsome black-haired, pink-cheeked young man who was young enough to be her grandson. The butcher himself was also astounded by this unexpected turn of affairs, and, on learning that Polly Malindy had ridden into town with Zeke, he would quickly lay aside his cleaver and take to his heels; so by the time she reached the butcher shop he was nowhere to be found. Not finding him, she would go up and down the few blocks that constituted Main Street, inquiring as to his whereabouts, and she often stayed in town all night, probably sleeping in her wagon, declaring she would "strike fer him agin in the mornin'." Eventually, this unrequited romance waned and died, and as age came more heavily upon her, she appeared less often in town, which was a disappointment to us children.

However, it was not long before another interesting inhabitant of the mountains came upon the scene. This was Old Man Ballew, who lived high among the further peaks not far from Mount Mitchell, which was the highest peak of all. My father enjoyed hunting and he had met Old Man Ballew on a hunting trip in the mountains, after which the old man invited him to go bear hunting with him and his sons. It was an interesting experience for my father to hunt with a group of hardy and experienced mountain men, especially since they used a famous breed of bear hunting dogs that had been bred by Big Tom Wilson, the most renowned bear hunter in the mountains of North Carolina and Tennessee. Big Tom Wilson had passed away before I was born, but the mountain people claimed "he couldn't in no ways be topped," and that "his name still rang." He had also gained extra recognition because it was he who had found the body of Professor Elisha Mitchell, for whom Mount Mitchell was named.

Professor Mitchell had set out one day in the long ago years to scale the peak that was later called by his name, but he did not return. Search parties were sent out in all directions to scour the mountain and learn what had become of him, but met without success. Then Big Tom Wilson was sent for, because he was known for his uncanny Indian-like ability for tracking game through the densest forests and over the roughest terrain.

It was said that his keen eye could catch any sign left by man or beast: a twig broken underfoot; a pebble or small rock dislodged from its place; a leafy branch pushed aside in a thicket; or the slightest impression made by a human or animal foot in a patch of moss. After trailing Professor Mitchell to the top of the peak and finding no trace of him, Big Tom started downward and it was then that he saw the professor's body lying in a clear, transparent pool of water below some rocks, from which he had fallen and drowned.

Old Man Ballew, who was full of stories about Big Tom Wilson, usually came to town during Court Week, along with other mountainfolk, and while there, he showed up at our house every day for the midday meal. In the mountains where he lived if one happened to be near the home of a friend at meal time, one simply stopped by to "break bread" with the family, knowing that no invitation was required, that "the latchstring hung on the outside" and a warm welcome awaited one. Unaware of mountain customs, but trained in village manners and amenities, Jim, our butler, said the old man "ought to take shame on hisself" for turning up uninvited, but when Old Man Ballew appeared, Jim always alerted Alice, our cook, and hastened to set an extra place on the table.

Like many other mountain men, Old Man Ballew was tall, rawboned, amazingly strong for his age, and of a majestic appearance. Although he had little schooling, he possessed a knowledge of man, beast and nature that could not be found in any book. He was highly respected for his integrity and it was said of him by the mountainfolk that he was "honest to a fault" and "as straight as a die."

My mother deplored the fact that he "slurped" his soup loudly and ate with his elbows on the table (for which offenses we children were made to leave the table), and she became nervous at times by the way he chewed tobacco and expectorated at will. It was fortunate that he did this out of doors, since my father did not chew tobacco or smoke and we had no cuspidors. However, he possessed a good deal of skill in the execution of this art, for he always spat with unerring aim. When seated on our front porch, he could select a spot on the other side of the driveway and he never missed his target.

I noticed that he had a peculiar way of positioning his mouth just before a blast-off, which, I felt, could give anyone time to duck, and since no mishaps occurred, in time my mother began to relax and to enjoy his mountain dialect and his quaint recitations of mountain lore. She also began to overlook his grammatical errors after he confessed that he had "a powerful strong leanin' toward the Lord." In fact, there were a few times when he was so moved by "the religious feelin' in my bosom" that he rose at the dinner table after my father had finished praying and said what he called "a extry grace prayer of my own," after which all of us felt we should say "Amen" again and did.

One of his peculiarities was the manner in which he wore his beard. Instead of letting it hang outside his homespun shirt, he kept it tucked inside, and there came a day when he felt called upon to rise to his feet and to address us in his somewhat ponderous but always deferential manner to explain the arrangement of this hirsute adornment.

"Beggin' yore pardon, but I'm tuck with a notion to surprise you-uns," he announced. "And betwixt you-uns and me and the gatepost, it jist might put you-uns in a wonder."

At this, he drew forth from the inside of his shirt what appeared to be an immaculately clean ball of white fluff that, as he unrolled it, turned out to be a long white beard that he had wrapped carefully about a corncob from which the kernels had been stripped.

"Me and Hiram Lowdermilk is a-runnin' a race betwixt us to find out which-uns' beard can be growed to the longest. I never was one to make a brag on myself, but I believe this-un has got his-un beat," he stated.

To our startled gaze, this appeared to be true, even though Hiram Lowdermilk was not on hand for comparison, for when he unrolled it, the beard reached the floor and lay a few inches thereupon; so we gave him our heartiest congratulations.

Strange as it may seem today, in my childhood there were still living amongst us many elderly persons who had been born in antebellum days before the Civil War and these so-called "ladies and gentlemen of the Old School" still clung to the manners, customs, and ethics of that earlier and more gracious time that had long since vanished and could never come again. Sometimes we were amused by their quaint, old-fashioned ways, but we held them in great respect, and it was from them that we learned of the Civil War and the Reconstruction Period and, young though we were, we became Confederates at heart.

On Confederate Memorial Day, the village had a parade and we children, led by the school superintendent and our teachers, marched from the schoolhouse on Green Street to the Courthouse Square, carrying bouquets of flowers for which every garden in town had been stripped. We placed the flowers at the base of the statue of the Confederate soldiers that stood upon the Courthouse lawn and as we did this we sang a song that began:

> *Low we lay our blossoms down,*
> *Like dew our tears,*
> *Brightly our warriors crown,*
> *And gleam through the years.*

Of course, everybody in town came to watch, and among them were many elderly ladies whose husbands, sons and sweethearts had been killed in the Civil War. They were dressed completely in mourning black and, we noted, they often shed tears and wiped their eyes with their handkerchiefs during the ceremony. There were also white haired old gentlemen who wore faded and worn Confederate uniforms, put on for the occasion; and some of them were without an arm or a leg, or were leaning on canes or crutches that they still needed because of ancient battle wounds.

Like most Southern children, I knew a list of Civil War battles when I was quite young. Robert E. Lee and Stonewall Jackson were our heroes and I was always asking elderly relatives for tales about the war and the times that preceded and followed it. These they told willingly because they wanted us to know and remember them.

In those days there stood near the center of town a number of large and handsome old homes that had been built before the Civil War and, like the old homes on the plantations in the valley, most of them had names. Our home, which stood on King Street only a few blocks from the Courthouse, had been built before the Civil War, and

# Chapter One

it was called Rose Villa because of its large rose garden. However, the rose garden that was most carefully and lovingly tended in town belonged to my father's half-aunt Claudia, who lived a block away. (This unusual relationship between them had come about because his Grandfather Holt had married twice and Aunt Claudia was his mother's half-sister.)

Aunt Claudia was really Mrs. Cameron Pearson. She was an elderly, childless widow who could tell many interesting stories about the Civil War, through which she had lived. She was a beautiful old lady, tiny, silver-haired, soft voiced, gentle and always immaculately dressed, often with lace ruffles at her throat and wrists. An added interest for us in the lady was that she had a secret that was known by the whole neighborhood, but she was unaware of this and no one would have dared to enlighten her.

The secret was that Emma, Aunt Claudia's cook, took to the whiskey bottle at times and sometimes even went on what was called "a dilly of a bender." At such times Aunt Claudia, not aware that the neighborhood knew exactly what was going on and hopeful of keeping it in ignorance, would say in her gentle and dignified way that Emma was "indisposed."

Sometimes the situation grew so bad that Aunt Claudia needed help, so she would telephone my mother and say, "Emma is indisposed. Will you be so kind as to send over Jim?"

On being alerted, Jim, who was the only person who seemed to know how to deal with Emma when she had had too much to drink, would stop whatever task to which he had been put under the stern eye of Alice, our cook. He would hasten out to the stable to get the wheelbarrow, and we children, knowing what was about to occur, would take off after him, our dogs at our heels, while he hurried to Aunt Claudia's—for the sake of propriety, using the back alley, of course.

Arriving at Aunt Claudia's back door, Jim, who was tall, thin, dignified, pious, a Life Deacon at Willow Tree Colored Baptist Church, and thought Emma's goings-on were "scandalous," would park the wheelbarrow close to the back steps and disappear into the house. Then a few minutes later, his face fixed in a scowl, he would emerge with Emma, who was always in excellent spirits, in need of a strong arm to lean upon, and delighted to find an appreciative audience awaiting her.

She would greet us happily, the scowling Jim being unable to get her to dispense with this formality before he could persuade her to be seated in the wheelbarrow. Then he would grab the handles of the wheelbarrow and set off at a trot down the alley while we jogged enthusiastically behind him, our canine escorts barking and frisking behind us. After following the alley for a short distance, he would turn to the right, down the hill toward Emma's house, the wheelbarrow bumping and bouncing over the ruts, and Emma would lurch this way and that—so that he would have to stop from time to time to straighten her up and keep her from tumbling out onto the ground. Sometimes she felt so happy that she sang, which added an extra fillip of excitement to the trip, but when we saw her a few days later she would appear as dignified and serene as Aunt Claudia herself—which made it difficult for us to believe that the ride in the wheelbarrow had ever taken place.

Farther down the street from Aunt Claudia lived another old lady who was as ugly as Aunt Claudia was beautiful. She, too, was a childless widow and, although we respectfully called her Mrs. Ray, she had a nickname that we thought was altogether unsuitable for one of her appearance and disposition. It was "La La," and to us it denoted a frivolity and attractiveness she did not possess. In fact, we decided that it must have been bestowed upon her by doting parents, who were charmed by her pattering baby footsteps and beguiling chatter in the long ago years and never dreamed that she would turn out as she had.

We children were a little afraid of her because we thought she looked like a witch. Dressed always in funereal black and leaning upon a gold-headed cane, she took her daily walk up and down our street and it would not have surprised us if the cane had suddenly changed into a broomstick and she had gone sailing off over the treetops.

She was said to be wealthy but "as tight as Dick's hatband," and she wore upon her head an ancient white wig that had turned greenish with age. She also had a vehement manner of speaking, pounding with her cane upon the floor when she wanted to drive home a point and at the same time shaking her head for emphasis.

The pounding of the cane and the head shaking caused the wig to slip steadily back upon her head until there was revealed to our fascinated gaze her shiny bald head, which had only a few bristly white hairs sticking up here and there upon it. Just as the wig was about to slip entirely off the back of her head, she would become aware of what was about to happen, but this did not cut off her flow of words or appear to embarrass her in the least. She would grab the wig and give it a quick shove forward, so that its front wavy portion would come to rest just above her large beaked nose, and the knot into which it was arranged at the back would stick up behind in a ridiculous fashion. The whole procedure would have caused us to go into paroxysms of laughter if we had not been afraid to laugh, and, while we restrained ourselves with difficulty, the entire process would be repeated again and again.

Sometimes I went to the old lady's house to spend the night with her great-niece, who came to visit her at times. On those occasions we two little girls slept in an upstairs bedroom next to the old lady's. One cold morning we were suddenly waked by the pounding of her cane upon the floor and her angry yells, summoning a niece with whom she lived to come to her aid. Frightened by the bedlam and curious as to the cause of it, we crept into the hall just as the niece sped past with an ice pick in her hand. The old lady's bedroom door stood open, which meant that we could look into her room and see the cause of the commotion.

Then we realized that, on going to bed the preceding night, she had followed her habit of hanging the greenish wig on a chair bedside her bed and placing her false teeth in a bowl of water on the seat of the chair. It had been a cold night and, since she always slept with her windows open, the water in the bowl had frozen, imprisoning the teeth. Consequently, in the morning when she reached for them her fingers encountered solidly frozen ice, which threw her into a tantrum.

While the niece chipped away determinedly with the ice pick in an attempt to free the teeth, the old lady kept thrashing about in the bed yelling, "Hurry up! Hurry Up! But don't you dare break my teeth!"

We realized that she must have been a little more attractive when the bloom of youth was upon her, and we were surprised to learn she once had actually had several suitors who wanted to marry her. Among them was a young gentleman who had varied from the usual way of proposing marriage to a lady and had written her instead, "addressing" her by letter. He wrote that if she looked with favor upon his suit, to let him know and he would come to the village at once—but that if he did not hear from her he would know that her answer was negative. Through a twist of fate, the letter was lost, and since she did not receive it, she wrote him no reply. Thinking she had rejected him, he did not put in an appearance and that was the end of that—at least, for the time being.

She married another man, who became an officer in the Confederate Army and, unfortunately, he had a leg shot off and had to wear a false one for the rest of his life. She lived with him many long years and when he died she grieved his passing with loud and prolonged lamentations accompanied by much head shaking, wig slipping and pounding of the cane upon the floor.

During the confusion incidental to his demise, she inadvertently overlooked the fact that he had been buried without his false leg and when she learned of this it sent her into an even more noisy exhibition of grief.

She stated the she would never feel that it was really he who was dead and buried because a part of him was not with him—that is, the false leg. She declared she had become so accustomed to the leg that it must be fetched from the attic, where it had been stored by some well meaning relative, and attached as it had been in life. Since she always had her way and did exactly as she pleased, we expected that this gruesome scheme would be attended to as speedily as possible, so we were surprised to learn that she finally gave in. The leg was allowed to remain in the attic, gathering dust, and the old gentleman was left to rest peacefully in his appointed place in the churchyard.

Many years later, when she was quite elderly, we were amazed to learn that the love letter in which the gentleman of an earlier day had asked her to marry him (but which she had not received) had at last come to light. It was found in the mail compartment of an ancient stagecoach, where it had slipped down into a crack and remained hidden throughout all the long years. We wondered about her emotions when she received it at last, but we decided that the gentleman she married must have been the right one for her after all, since it would have been impossible for her to mourn any spouse with longer, louder, and more violent lamentations than she had exhibited at his passing.

Since life had flowed along at the same leisurely pace—with a few unusual occurrences from time to time—we felt it would continue in the same way indefinitely. However, almost before we were aware of it, an event took place that was to change the village and its environs so greatly that they would never be the same again.

## Chapter Two

*Gasoline Machines — The Stagecoach — The Train —
Miss Maggie Jenks — The Sea Captain and His Lady —
Mary Louise and Elizabeth Matilda — Two Tragic
Romances — Edward*

### 2.

The event that made such a big impact on the life in the little town and changed it forever was the coming of the automobile. However, these gasoline propelled monsters that began to invade our quiet, tree-shaded, unpaved streets were not called automobiles. At first they were referred to as gasoline machines and later on as machines.

Horses and mules, on glimpsing them heading their way, sputtering and coughing, followed by clouds of dust or splashing mud and water in all directions, plunged and reared in terror. Sometimes they even overturned the vehicles to which they were attached, spilling passengers willy-nilly along the way, or broke from between the shafts and galloped wildly off into the distance. The pandemonium that resulted was made still worse by the shrieks and yells of frightened passersby and the barking of all the dogs in the area—while many men and boys set off running at top speed to catch the fleeing animals.

When my father, who had an adventurous spirit, bought one of the first gasoline machines brought to town for sale, my mother was aghast and certain that some catastrophe would surely result. As for my father's two elderly maiden sisters Mary Louise and Matilda, who lived at their old ancestral home in the country, they stated that they would never under any circumstance purchase one of the dangerous new contraptions and they never did. They also refused to set foot in my father's gasoline machine for quite a long time.

However, there were other villagers who considered themselves to be "more forward thinking in their ideas," and they stated that, with the coming of the gasoline machines, progress was being made.

They remembered that the railroad had not been brought all the way to town until after the Civil War. It had stopped about six miles away at a place called "the head of the road" and persons who traveled to any distance had to go by stagecoach, but after the railroad was brought all the way to town, the stagecoach was abandoned.

Then the train was quickly accepted as the best mode of travel and they predicted that, as it had been with the train, so would it be with gasoline machines.

I had been interested in learning that my aunts, who were girls during the Civil War, had traveled to school at Saint Mary's Episcopal Female Academy at Raleigh in a stagecoach drawn by six beautiful white horses. It had a trumpeter who sat atop it beside the driver and trumpeted its arrivals and departures. The tune he played was a rollicking melody called "Dumplings for Dinner." I thought such rides must have been delightful, but my aunts said that the train was definitely an improvement over the swaying, jolting, jerking stagecoach.

I was also interested in knowing that at first the train was called "the cars," and the engine that pulled them was often jokingly referred to as "the iron horse." They told me "the cars" ran on a very elastic schedule at first, for the engineer, on request, would allow them to linger at stations along the way (later called depots). This was to enable those on board to descend to the station platform to meet friends who had gathered there (and in early days a crowd of villagers usually assembled to greet visitors and see who was on board). Thus, often a reception of sorts took place with much chatter, laughter, and shaking of hands. Also as the villagers became more accustomed to the cars and the iron horse that pulled them, they began "taking the cars" (as boarding the train was called), going to visit friends and relatives in other places and just taking trips.

One of the first trains that rattled into Morganton brought to the village a tall, dark and handsome young man named William E. Powe of South Carolina, and thereby hangs a romantic tale that I enjoyed when I was a child. Shortly after his arrival, he was seen by a red haired charmer, Miss Catherine Elvira Tate, the daughter of a prominent doctor in the community.

After taking a look at the unsuspecting young man, the young lady said to the two friends who were with her, "I don't know who that man is, but he's the one I'm going to marry."

It happened that they met at a ball that night and she married him six months later. She was a relative of my father and many years later, when I was a child and she an elderly lady, I came to know her well and was devoted to her. By then, her husband had passed away and her red hair had turned to a silvery white, but she had retained the charm that had ensnared the young man, and she was one of the most popular and respected persons in town.

## Chapter Two

Before the turning of the century, another important event occurred and this was the establishment of a plant for generating electricity. I cannot remember a time when we did not have telephones and electric lights in the village, but I was told that when electricity was first available, the lights were cut off at midnight. At eleven-thirty they began to blink, signalling the cut-off and giving the villagers time to prepare for bed.

There were persons on our street who waited for the blinks to tell them when to go to bed. When it was announced that in the future the electric lights would stay on all night, Miss Sue Tate and her two maiden sisters, Miss Irene and Miss Wilhelmina, obviously forgot about the new rule and sat up all night, waiting for the blinks that never came. Finally, realizing that something was amiss, they opened the shutters at a window, found that the sun was shining and morning had come—which caused some amusement in our neighborhood.

As for the telephones of that day, they were rather small square black metal boxes that hung on walls and one had only to lift the receiver and ask Central, an unseen lady who had them in charge, to ring the number one wanted. The telephones in the country were not like those in town, however. They, too, were constructed to hang on walls, but they were made of oak wood with projecting mouthpieces and cranks on the side that had to be wound up to alert the country Central—who was simply called by her name, which, if I remember correctly, happened to be Maybelle.

She was much more approachable and friendly than the town Central, and she knew everyone on the country line, as well as everything there was to know about them. She "listened in" when she desired to do so, broke in on conversations to add information, ask questions or give advice when she felt it was needed, and was so pleasant and agreeable that no one minded. When other persons "listened in," however, it was considered to be very bad manners and even unethical. When my two aunts who lived in the country could tell by certain sounds along the line that they had listeners, they found this annoying, for listeners also weakened the voices of those who were having a conversation.

Once when Aunt Matilda was talking to a friend and heard a rooster crowing she asked, "Is that your rooster crowing?" When told it was not, she replied, "Well, it's certainly not mine!" And, at that, she could hear receivers being hung up along the line.

Not long after the electric light system was established, an ice plant was also built and the enclosed ice wagon with "ICE" painted in big letters on each side and drawn by a patient, plodding mule that we children called the Ice Mule, was seen upon our streets. The Ice Man had to drive the Ice Wagon slowly, keeping on the outlook for the placards of white cardboard that hung at front doors along the way, for on them was printed in large black numerals the number of pounds of ice that were needed at the different homes.

At homes needing ice, he drove his wagon as close as possible to the back doors, sawed off the correct number of pounds from the huge block of ice in the wagon, and then swung them up with a pair of large iron tongs into the ice compartments on top of ice boxes. The ice boxes were chests made of oak wood and were about four or five feet in height and had interiors lined with zinc that contained shelves upon which food could be kept chilled.

Although the villagers knew that the little town could never regain the wealth and prestige of the past, they found satisfaction in the coming of the train and the installment of telephones and electric lights. They also took pleasure in the few streets that had been paved, and after the horses and mules became accustomed to the gasoline machines and the streets were peaceful again, they decided that things were really going along in a better fashion than they had expected. Therefore, they began to prophecy that more productive times lay ahead—which was to turn out to be true, but the pain, heartbreak and grinding poverty through which they had passed could not easily be forgotten.

With so many men killed in the Confederate Army, it had been upon the Southern widows that the burden of rearing, feeding, clothing and educating the children had fallen. Elvira Erwin, like other Southern women who lived on plantations, had been hard pressed to keep the place running after the death of Joseph Erwin, who died not long after the Civil War. Bloody Kirk, the mountain raiders and the Yankee Army had taken all the horses and mules, leaving only colts not yet fit for the plow. Most of the black people had left the place except for those who had decided to remain. The rich fields in the bottom lands along the river and creek were growing up in weeds and brambles, which brought want and starvation closer day by day. Needing money but having none (for Confederate money was useless and could buy nothing), with what frustration and hopelessness Elvira must have looked down from the once happy old home on the hill across the desolate land.

## Chapter Two

Poverty stricken white families had begun to come down from the mountains to work in the valleys and in these Elvira Erwin found her first hope. Like others in her situation, she established the tenant system, in which they could work the land "on shares" along with the remaining black people, and slowly under her management the weed choked acres began to yield.

At the time of her husband's death, my father, the youngest of her ten living children, was only eleven years old and she despaired over getting education for her children. There still were few schools for white children in the South and the North was not willing to offer money for the establishment of white schools, as it had for schools for the black children.

In a few years, however, she found hope in the fact that, due to the lack of white schools and also the lack of money to establish new ones, there had come into existence a few schools for boys that were called "self help schools." At these schools, a good education could be attained and the students paid for their schooling by "working in the fields and bringing in the crops." On hearing of a highly rated school of this type over the mountains in Tennessee, Elvira sent to it her oldest son, young William Allen Erwin, and this proved to be one of the smartest decisions of her life.

William was tall for his age, quick and strong, and unusually bright. Later he was to become a handsome and impressive man six feet and four inches tall. Best of all he was eager to learn, willing to work and ready for labor of any sort. In remembering his mother's decision to send him to the school in Tennessee, I remember also a letter that he wrote to her while he was a student there, a boyish note that touches my heart even now.

I found it in a cupboard at Bellevue when I was a small girl visiting at the old home. I took it to my aunts and we read it together. We were touched by the promise William made to his mother and also by the abundant manner in which he fulfilled it later on.

"Dear Mother," he wrote. "Please don't worry about anything. When I'm a man I'm going to work hard and give you everything you want."

After William finished his schooling in Tennessee Elvira somehow scraped up enough money to send him to a business school for a few years, at which he showed great capability, and after that to the well-known Holt Plaid Mills at Burlington, North Carolina, that were owned by several of her Holt uncles.

The Holts had been early pioneers in the cotton manufacturing business. They were making money, becoming wealthy and well-known throughout the South. They quickly recognized the ability of their young kinsman and for more than a decade he served as treasurer and manager of the Holt Plaid Mills at Burlington.

When Ben Duke of tobacco manufacturing fame decided to move into textile manufacturing, according to the printed record "he showed great talent in picking the right man for the job — thirty-six year old William Allen Erwin — to establish and manage the new textile mill." The record also states that when William Erwin informed his former employers that he was leaving they let him go with the greatest reluctance and paid him high tribute. (from The Dukes of Durham by Durden)

L. Banks Holt declared that "in a life one seldom finds an all round man, which he considered William Erwin to be." He told Duke that "the young man had extensive business capacity, was utterly reliable, as true as steel and withal a Christian gentleman." Holt added, "I cannot part with him without saying that I cannot find words that will express too strongly my good opinion of him."

When the time came to select a name for the new mill that was to be established the lawyer in the case said, "Let us name it for this young man (Erwin). Then if it fails the onus will be on him and if it succeeds it will be his glory."

The mill, which was built in Durham, North Carolina, succeeded beyond all hopes and expectations, as did the other numerous mills William Erwin established in other places throughout the state. Under his expert management it was not long before the roar of the looms and the singing of the hundreds of whirling spindles in the mills combined in a song of wealth and prosperity in which all members of the extensive and close knit family shared, including the two maiden sisters at the old home on the hill and "William Erwin became one of the wealthiest and most prominent men in the South."

The maiden sisters continued to live at the old home throughout the years while all of their brothers and sisters married and moved away to homes of their own in other places. As time passed, William's three younger brothers — James Locke, Jesse Harper and Joseph Ernest — joined him in managing the mills. However, regardless of how far away they lived they and their married sisters never failed to go to Bellevue as often as possible and I was always impressed by how much they enjoyed being there and how much pleasure they took in the company of each other.

## Chapter Two

My father was the only one of the brothers and sisters who settled in Morganton, where he operated two large mills in the Erwin chain. I have always been glad that he did this, for it enabled me to visit at Bellevue more often and to know my aunts Mary Louise and Matilda more intimately than any of the other numerous grandchildren. It also enabled me to enjoy hearing the ladies tell many of the stories I have included in this collection of tales.

Before I was born, the more adventurous citizens had begun "to take the cars" in increasing numbers, and, to the joy of the villagers, the cars had also begun bringing travelers to town in increasing numbers, too. These were mostly persons who were trying to escape the summer heat in the eastern part of the state and wanted to enjoy the fine climate that Morganton offered, as well as the beautiful mountain scenery.

As these vacationers continued to arrive, and even grew in numbers, certain far-seeing persons saw in this a financial opportunity of which no one had dreamed. It began to appear that Morganton was on its way to being a small summer resort—which it had already become by the time I was a child.

In the town were a number of elderly widows and maiden ladies who lived in fine and large old homes they found hard to support and they decided to take in boarders during the summer months. They were not called boarders, however. They were referred to as "summer guests," and at first they were hand picked, blue-blooded friends or friends of friends—"persons one would not find uncongenial in one's home."

Among these far seeing ladies was one who lived on our street in a large old home where the Episcopal rectory now stands. She was called Miss Maggie Jenks, although she was really Mrs. Walton, and she was one of the blue-bloods of the town. I do not remember how her unusual mixture of names came about, but she was energetic and enterprising and her boarding house soon became popular.

Miss Maggie Jenks had a grown son named Jack who helped her to run the place, and he had a beautiful Irish Setter, that, surprisingly, was also named Jack. In order to keep the two apart in our minds, we children called the son Mr. Jack and the Irish setter Dog Jack and we became quite fond of both. Mr. Jack had trained Dog Jack to go for the mail every morning right after the train came in, so directly after breakfast, rain or shine, we would see Dog Jack loping down our street headed for the post office in the center of town, where the postmaster, who was expecting him, handed him a neatly tied bundle of mail. Then, a little later, he would come loping back, carrying the bundle in his mouth.

This early and prompt delivery of the mail increased the popularity of Miss Maggie Jenks' boarding house so much, that after a few years had gone by she was emboldened to slip in amongst her blue-blooded and aristocratic guests a maverick or two of whom no one in town had ever heard. At first, this was a shock to the other ladies in the neighborhood, regardless of how many extra shekels it brought to hand; but it could not be denied that these unknown aliens who had sought out our quiet town caused everyone to take more interest in the boarding house and also quickened the tempo of village life.

One of them was a tall and handsome old gentleman who walked with a military step and spoke with a guttural German accent. He had a mustache waxed into points that stood up on each side of his nose, pointing skyward, and he looked so much like the German General von Hindenburg, whose picture had often been in the newspapers during the First World War, that we children stood a little in awe of him, thinking that perhaps he was a German spy.

He took his daily walk up and down our street, sounding like a big bumblebee as he hummed a certain tune. When we asked the name of the song, he said it was called "The Watch on the Rhine," and when we asked his name, he said something that sounded like Near God; so that was what we called him—Mr. Near God. He came to Miss Maggie Jenks' boarding house for several summers, then disappeared as suddenly as he had appeared, which made us feel that he might really have been a German spy after all—although there did not seem to be a need for one since the First World War had been over for several years.

Another interesting gentleman who caught our attention was an elderly sea captain, who was not tall and imposing like Mr. Near God, but short and so bandy legged that it was hard to imagine his keeping his balance on the deck of a tossing schooner when a sou'wester was at its worst. He, too, had a mustache, but it was of the walrus type and hung down below his chin—as though he might be trying to make up for his diminutive size by this impressive hirsute adornment.

He brought with him his wife—a white-haired, delightful little lady who was as bright-eyed as a robin but so crippled with arthritis that she spent her days in a wheelchair, wrapped in silk scarves and shawls. A trained nurse in a starched white uniform and cap rolled the wheelchair up and down our street, and the little captain often marched beside it, stroking his luxuriant whiskers from time to time and chatting with his wife, whom he appeared to adore.

At first, the ladies on our street stood somewhat aloof from this unusual pair—until a tale began to circulate about a romance of an unusual order that related in a dramatic way to Napoleon Bonaparte and his younger brother Jerome. Jerome Bonaparte had married the beautiful and well born Betsy Patterson of Baltimore while on a trip to the United States, but had deserted her and their little son when Napoleon repudiated the marriage. There had been quite a lot written about this romance and marriage in the newspapers at the time, so the ladies, remembering this, soon became eager to meet the captain's wife, for the tale was told that she was a close relative of the ill-fated Betsy. And what could be more interesting, they felt, than to get the full story with all the details straight from the horse's mouth, as it were?

Accordingly, the couple began receiving invitations to afternoon tea parties at homes up and down the street, and the little captain came along to help the trained nurse lift the wheelchair onto shady summer porches or into parlors kept cool by blinds closed against the sun, after which the conversations went along at a brisk and delightful rate while the tea cakes, lemonade or iced tea were served.

Although the little silk-swathed, rheumatic wife was the main attraction, the sea captain soon became well liked, too. In some way, it had leaked out that the family of the wife, being prominent and wealthy, had looked down upon the captain because he came from a lowly background and was poor. However, in spite of this, the couple had eloped and sailed happily away. Although her family promptly disinherited her, they had continued to sail on, she always accompanying him on his voyages, and through the years they had cast anchor at many faraway and exotic ports—always blissfully happy and always together.

Since they had no children, this lifestyle continued until they became elderly and the wife grew too lame from rheumatism to accompany him. The captain loved his wife so dearly, however, that he left the sea and spent his time caring for and continuing to adore her. At the thought of this, certain ladies who were romantically inclined were touched by the very thought of such devotion and even blinked back a tear or two. Nor was this all. When they got the captain to talking, they were enthralled by the tales he could tell of distant countries and islands the pair had visited and of which they themselves had never even heard. Consequently, before that first summer was over they began to like and admire the captain, too, and some even spoke of him as "a man of parts"—which was high praise in those days.

Although the whole town took an interest in the increasing number of "summer guests," there were two visitors to town who were not in this category. They came often all the year round but stayed briefly, and mostly on Sundays; and these were my father's two older maiden sisters, Mary Louise and Elizabeth Matilda. They lived at their old ancestral home in the country about four miles from town and came in on Sundays to attend Grace Episcopal Church, of which both were staunch members. In the early days of my childhood they rode in a surrey that had a fringed top and was driven by kind old black Uncle Ike, who had been their father's coachman before the Civil War. (We children were taught to call all elderly black people "uncle" and "aunt" and to treat them with respect.)

Incidentally, when Uncle Ike, the two sisters, and other elderly persons, both white and black, spoke of "the war" they meant the Civil War, although other wars had been fought in the years since it ended.

Anyone, on meeting the two ladies, could tell at a glance that they were as unalike as two sisters could be. Both were in their sixties (which was considered to be quite an old age at that time). Aunt Mary Lou, who was two years older than Aunt Matilda, was tall and slender. Her face was thin. Her nose was long and she wore her grey hair parted in the middle and brushed smoothly back into a knot at the back of her head.

Unlike Aunt Matilda, who was interested in the fashions, Aunt Mary Lou paid little attention to the styles and usually wore dresses of black silk taffeta and small black hats with little decoration. In fact, the only way in which the sisters were alike was in wearing their skirts to the floor, even after hems crept up to the knee—which both ladies thought was "scandalous."

Aunt Mary Lou had a manner of speaking that was pleasant but always dignified and she possessed none of the attractions that were a part of Aunt Matilda's repertoire of charms: the trilling laughter; the quick but graceful gestures of her plump be-ringed hands; and the nods and smiles that added emphasis to the glances of her sparkling dark eyes. However, these allurements were not missed in Aunt Mary Lou by those of us who loved her, knew her well, and could take her true measure.

When I look back across the years and think of Aunt Matilda, I see her most often wearing a dress of plum colored silk and a plum colored bonnet adorned by a plum colored ostrich plume that dipped and quivered every time she turned her head; and I know that under the bonnet her carefully waved silver hair was coiled like the crown of a queen on the top of her head. In the sunlight the plum color of the dress and bonnet lent a delicate but becoming tint to her girlishly smooth and fair complexion, upon which she lavished great care and which she kept through the long years almost until the day she died.

Her small but plump, carefully manicured hands were squeezed into too-tight white kid gloves through which her rings could be seen poking up; for it was her boast that she could still wear the same size glove and shoe she wore when she was a young and slender girl—although we felt that she would have been more comfortable if her vanity would have allowed her to wear both in a larger size. She was several inches shorter than the tall and slender Aunt Mary Lou and had grown somewhat stout with the passing of the years, but she was still considered to be a very handsome lady and she never seemed to lose the ability to catch the eye of some elderly gentleman.

When she and Aunt Mary Lou came in to church on Sunday mornings, there was often some courtly old gentleman who stepped forward to greet her, to accompany her into the vestibule of the church and to turn her over to an admiring usher, who escorted her to the family pew, which was second from the front on the right hand side. Behind her trailed Aunt Mary Lou, dressed, as usual, in black, her only adornment being an old-fashioned "mourning brooch" of black onyx that she wore on Sundays, the sort of brooch worn by ladies of her generation when in mourning for the deceased (for when a lady was in bereavement, any jewelry that glistened or shone was taboo). In front, the brooch had a little glass window through which could be glimpsed the entwined locks of hair of her departed parents. Upon her head sat a simple black hat and on her face there was what we called her "worshipping look"—reverent and apart; as if, on entering the church, she had cast all earthly thoughts aside and the words of the Prayer Book were already flowing into her mind.

She sang the hymns and chants in church in a thin, high, soprano, sometimes on key and sometimes off, and she seemed to enjoy particularly the Venite, Exultemus, Domino, which she went through with unflagging determination:

> *O come, let us sing unto the Lord:*
> *Let us heartily rejoice in the strength of our salvation:*
> *Let us come before His presence with Thanksgiving;*
> *And show ourselves glad in Him with psalms.*

Aunt Matilda, on the other hand, gave forth with a rich and vibrant alto that never for an instant strayed in the wrong direction. She was the only lady I knew who sang alto and I considered this to be a rare distinction. In the tints of blue, rose, and gold that fell athwart the family pew from a stained glass window nearby, the sisters sank upon their knees in prayer on the kneeling bench, which, like the pew, was comfortably cushioned. It was Aunt Matilda who saw to that. She said she was not like Aunt Mary Lou, "who seemed to want to mortify the flesh." She believed that one should be as comfortable in the House of the Lord as anywhere else and, when a person had rheumatism, kneeling on a hard, uncushioned board was somewhat painful, to say the least.

In spite of my love and admiration for my aunts, at an early age I began to feel that there must be something about them that was amiss, for unlike their eight brothers and sisters, they had no husbands or offspring. My mother had impressed upon me the fact that questions were rude, so I held my peace. However, as time went by I came upon bits of information that, pieced together, fortunately threw a little light upon this puzzling situation.

Sometimes when elderly female relatives drank tea about a parlor fire, I was fascinated by enlightening statements they let fall about family matters, and there were times on summer porches after dark when the shadows that hid the ladies seemed to encourage a more personal exchange of confidences than they permitted themselves by the light of day. On such occasions the squeak of their rocking chairs, as rhythmic as the rise and fall of their palm leaf fans, punctuated their softly spoken sentences and filled the pregnant little silences in between, and it was then that, little by little, I learned of the tragic romances of my two maiden aunts.

I found that Aunt Matilda, who was known as a belle in her youth, had a number of suitors and had selected one who lived in another town and was handsome, charming, well born and suitable in every way. I also learned that courting was carried out under difficulties in her youthful years, for in those days a gentleman who wished to "pay attention" to a lady had to request this privilege from "the male head of her family." "Paying attention" meant calling upon the lady, presenting her with "appropriate" gifts such as a bouquet of flowers, a box of candy or a book, and escorting her to social affairs that did not take place at a distance. Any event that involved transportation to a distance required that a chaperon be in attendance and this meant a married lady of impeccable reputation. No spinster, regardless of how circumspect and highly regarded she might be, was considered to be suitable for this task.

If all went well, as time passed by, the gentleman had another talk with the "male head of the family" to discuss certain serious matters that had not been touched upon before, and to request the privilege of "addressing" her (that is, of "popping the question" as it was called in that day). If this was granted, he then "addressed" her and if she accepted him, it was considered to be proper for him to give her a more elaborate gift, which was often a sterling silver comb and brush set. The more expensive of these sets included, along with the comb and brush, a hand mirror, a shoe horn, a pin tray, and a cut glass "hair receiver" with a silver top in which a lady could keep combings of her hair that could be made into a long and fashionable hairpiece, called a "switch," that could be arranged upon her head in the manner she desired.

Although engagements often were not announced right away, the news usually leaked out and everyone was aware that the couple had what was called "an understanding." After an interval, when they decided to make an announcement, the gentleman gave her an engagement ring and also an engagement gift—which was usually a piece of jewelry, often a brooch. This interesting series of events naturally led to a wedding, but the usual engagement lasted at least a year while some lasted much longer.

Incidentally, there were only three times during a lady's life when it was thought to be proper for her name to appear in a newspaper or journal of any sort for the public to read. These were when she was born, when she was married, and when she died. For it to appear in print at any other time was considered to be in bad taste and was taboo.

In time and in the manner I have described, I finally learned that

Aunt Matilda and her chosen suitor had gone through a proper courtship and the young gentleman had "addressed her." They had reached "an understanding" and become engaged, but during the absence of her beloved, Aunt Matilda's natural interest in young gentlemen led her to "receive attention" from another masculine admirer, who also wanted to marry her. Boiled down to actual facts, she had allowed him to escort her from a party in town to the home of her uncle, where she was visiting at the time. When her chosen one learned of this, he became angry and jealous and reprimanded her sharply but, as accustomed as she was to "wrapping young gentlemen about her little finger," she tossed her dark curls and told him she intended to do exactly as she pleased.

She thought, of course, that he would get over his anger and return, but he did not. Instead, he began to pay attention to a cousin of hers, who looked like her but was not so charming and pretty, and according to the relative who related the story, the cousin "snapped him up quicker than you could say 'cat'."

This relative also told me she was present when he and Aunt Matilda came face to face for the first time after his wedding and she said with emphasis, "He was visibly affected—visibly affected!" His marriage, which was childless, turned out to be unhappy, but in those days there was nothing that could be done about it. In fact, this relative confided that, "To be divorced was to be in disgrace, and, well, it just simply wasn't done."

This being the case, the gentleman and his wife lived together unhappily through the years and Aunt Matilda lived on with Aunt Mary Lou in the big brick house on the hill. She continued to receive attention from gentlemen from time to time (a number of whom "addressed" her), but she never allowed these friendships to reach the stage of "an understanding" and she never fell in love with another man. She kept the photographs of her suitors in the big album bound in mother-of-pearl on a certain table in the parlor, it being the fashion of the day to keep albums on parlor tables, and when I was a small girl visiting the aunts and it was too rainy to go out and play, she would often open the album.

"Child," she would say, "if you'll be nice and quiet, I'll let you sit beside me and look at the photographs of my suitors."

Then, while the rain pattered against the window panes, we would sit together, absorbed in the pictures inserted into the openings in the thick yellowed pages of the album. Such an assortment of whiskers I had never seen before. There were goatees, pointed and rounded; sideburns, some cropped short and others flaring; walrus mustaches; mutton chops; mustaches that hung down like bicycle handlebars; and even a full beard that was cut square at the bottom like a spade.

As we sat together and Aunt Matilda's plump be-ringed fingers turned the pages, we examined each gentleman in turn and sometimes she told me stories about them—but never about him, although it was about him that I really wanted to know. He was the handsomest of the lot and after scrutinizing his photographs (and there were several) I came to feel that I knew the manner of man he was; for she sometimes let fall hints that I could piece together into the sort of gentleman who I thought could win her heart.

She said she couldn't abide a man who was "big footed and awkward," that she liked a man to have a "neat, well shod foot and a well kept hand" and that she admired especially a man who was graceful in his movements and had courtly manners. She also stated that she once had a suitor who owned a beautiful black horse with a coat that shone like satin and the finest silver mounted harness she had ever seen.

From these and other hints she let fall, he took form and stood before me—tall, trim and as handsome as Sir Lockivar—having just dashed up to Aunt Matilda's door on a beautiful black horse with the finest silver mounted harness that one could ever hope to see. Several years later when I met him, I saw a distinguished looking, silver haired, courtly old gentleman with a trim figure, who was not so tall as I had imagined him to be. He had fine aristocratic features, but there was something that was missing about him—as though some spring inside him had come unwound and he was slowly running down. One could glimpse it in his faded blue eyes that had none of the sparkle of Aunt Matilda's. Certainly nothing about Aunt Matilda had broken down or become unwound, and, if she had ever "carried a torch" for the gentleman, as some persons seemed to think, it had flickered low during the years and had even gone out. Instead, as we pored over the album she seemed to take only a nostalgic pride in the siren she once had been.

As for Aunt Mary Lou, she had no photographs of her beloved on display, but I learned that the gentleman of her choice had journeyed all the way to Morganton from his home in Baltimore to gain her father's blessing upon the match and to "address her." However, according to the tale, he stopped en route overnight at the inn in the village and made a "grievous mistake."

According to the relative who told me this sad story, "He unadvisedly took too much spirits and became somewhat intoxicated."

Perhaps he was only trying to prime himself for "addressing her," but when the news reached her father, who never drank spirituous liquors, he said he'd rather see one of his daughters in her grave than married to a drunkard, and in this opinion he was said to be justified, since one of his nieces was in that predicament at the time. To Aunt Mary Lou and her sisters, Pa was the embodiment of all that was perfection in a man, and, in view of this, the romance was quickly ended. The suitor went back to Baltimore and Aunt Mary Lou, like Aunt Matilda, never fell in love again.

After her blighted romance, Aunt Matilda, never one to be worsted in any situation, busied herself with entertaining relatives and friends at Bellevue and attending social events in town and at other old homes in the valley. Following her mother's death, she took over the housekeeping and soon gained the reputation of being a notable hostess. What she enjoyed most of all, however, was keeping Open House at all times for her brothers and sisters and their families who were continuously trooping to the old home as happily as Muslims trekking to Mecca.

Aunt Mary Lou, who was of a more serious and religious turn of mind, sought solace in a different way. The family noticed that she began to read her Bible and Prayer Book more often and said her prayers more often, too. Also, there were nights when she had not finished praying before going to bed but Aunt Matilda had already finished her prayers and was ready to blow out the lamp and jump under the covers. To speak, or even whisper to anyone who was still communing with the Almighty was considered to be irreverent; so Aunt Matilda would slip downstairs to report to Pa that Mary Lou was praying too long again.

At this, Pa would mount the stairs, touch his eldest daughter gently and lovingly upon the shoulder and say sympathetically, "Go to bed now, daughter. It's time to go to bed."

Mary Lou would rise from her knees, blow out the lamp and get into the big walnut sleigh bed beside her sister, where the two would lie in the darkness, together and yet apart, each with her own different thoughts, memories, hopes, and dreams of the future—a future in which they managed to live altogether different lives under the same roof in the same old house on the hill.

The sisters rarely mentioned their tragic romances in my presence, but when they did, it was at a time when I was visiting them and they were preparing for bed. At that late hour after the day was spent, their conversations somehow reminded me of the last sleepy twittering of birds in the nest at the fall of night. They understood each other perfectly, but what they said was often incomprehensible to me, for their sentences were shorter, with silences in between, and sometimes they even spoke in monosyllables.

"June sixth . . ." Aunt Matilda murmured one night as she went behind the dressing screen in their bedroom to undress, from where I could hear her sigh with relief as she loosened her stays and took off her corset.

"I remember," replied Aunt Mary Lou.

"So I thought," said Aunt Matilda.

"How could I forget, Matilda—when it was the night Edward addressed you?"

Aunt Matilda came out from behind the dressing screen, yielding it to Aunt Mary Lou. "A lovely June night . . ." she said.

"Just like this—everything the same—except for the mockingbird," added Aunt Mary Lou.

"The mockingbird?" repeated Aunt Matilda.

"That sang in the magnolia tree close to the parlor window. Don't you remember?"

"Of course I do!" declared Aunt Matilda. "It made such a racket on moonlit nights I couldn't sleep a wink."

"I thought it was beautiful, like a nightingale. I used to lie awake just to listen," said Aunt Mary Lou.

"Oh, for goodness sakes, Mary Lou!"

"Sometimes even now, I seem to hear it in my dreams," responded Aunt Mary Lou.

"Dreaming of a bird! And after all we've been through!" exclaimed Aunt Matilda. "The war was bad enough and what came after was even worse."

"But sometimes I can't help looking back and remembering." Aunt Mary Lou went to the window and looked out at the full moon and the star filled sky. She hesitated a moment and then said, "Sometimes I fear you sent Edward away too hastily, Matilda."

In the soft yellow glow of lamplight that filled the room, Aunt Matilda went to the bureau and started putting crimping pins in her hair, so that it would curl the right way in the morning.

"I know you think I should have gone running right back and made up with him," Aunt Matilda replied. "But I'm glad I found out just in time what a jealous nature and quick temper he had."

Aunt Mary Lou sighed, waiting at the window and looking out into the night, as though it held her in its moon-white spell. "But you made such a perfect match. Everyone said so. He had addressed you and Pa had even given you his blessing."

She sighed again, while the curtains of Nottingham lace began to stir in the cool night breeze that was beginning to creep up the hill from the river. Then she added, speaking more softly than before, "I hear that Augusta hasn't been at all well, and sometimes I even have the feeling that if something should happen . . . " she paused and added hastily, "but, of course, I wish poor Augusta no harm."

"You mean to say you really think Edward would come running back and address me after all these years? Have you lost your senses, Mary Lou?"

Aunt Matilda put on her nightcap and tied the ribbons under her chin with a jerk while Aunt Mary Lou remained standing at the window, looking out into the night. I looked out, too, and saw that the moon was round and golden and a few low hanging stars seemed to be caught again in the topmost boughs of the big hemlock tree down by the front gate.

"It was you he loved," Aunt Mary Lou said softly. "Not Augusta."

"Well, he married her!" Aunt Matilda retorted.

When the sisters came to town on Sundays to go to church, they always lingered to take what we called Sunday Dinner at our house. It was a bountiful meal, served piping hot and ready for the table the moment we reached home. However, as much of it as possible had been prepared the preceding day because my parents believed that Sunday was a day of worship and rest, and in these the servants should share. After dinner the sisters lingered a little longer to discuss the news they had learned from relatives and friends at church.

Then, as soon as the servants had eaten and the kitchen was tidied, we would see Ginny Mule, hitched to Jim's cart, starting down our front driveway with Jim and Alice on the plank seat in front and Jane and Cathun in the back perched on kitchen chairs borrowed for the occasion—all of them dressed in their "Sunday-go-to-meetin' clothes" and headed for Willow Tree Colored Baptist Church several miles up the river.

When the ladies were ready to start for home, they would often invite me to go with them for a little visit and when I was permitted to go I was overjoyed, for going to the old brick home on the hill in the valley was like going back in time to an altogether different and more delightful world.

*A Visit to a Different World — Hat Tubs — Featherbeds — Chemises — The Chicken Thief — The Ten Commandments — The Crazy Woman — When the Kitchen Caught Fire — The Chemise That Could Fly — The High Buggy and the Low Buggy — Good Manners*

3.

Like other old homes on the plantations in the valley, the home of my aunts had a name. It was called Bellevue (beautiful view) and it stood on a high hill four miles outside town overlooking a wide stretch of bottom land along the river and the creek, the forests beyond and the faraway mountains, whose peaks reached forever upward into the wide blue arch of the sky.

In my early childhood when I first began to visit there, the State Rural Electrification System had not been established, so there could be no electricity in the house and, of course, no running water. Water for all purposes had to be drawn from a well that stood close to the back door under a well house that had a peaked roof.

At night, light was furnished by kerosene lamps and each morning the glass chimneys of these lamps had to be cleaned and the wicks trimmed, a task that no servant enjoyed. The lamps in the parlor and sitting room were larger and more elaborate in design than those used in the bedrooms and they had wide flaring shades that stood well away from the chimneys— a precaution to keep them from catching fire. Some of these shades were fluted and some had scenery or flowers painted on them.

Because of the lack of electricity, there was no heat in the house except that furnished by fires in the fireplaces, which were in every room, and since there was no running water, there were no bathrooms.

Aunt Matilda yearned for a bathroom like those in town, which had big white bathtubs that stood on ball and claw feet several inches off the floor, but, since this was not possible, she had to make do with hat tubs instead. Hat tubs were made of tin and looked like huge hats with wide flaring brims and, when in use, they appeared to be enormous hats resting upside down upon the floor—that is, upon their crowns. There were two hat tubs at Bellevue and every spring they were freshly painted. Sometimes they were pale pink, sometimes pale green or lavender, depending upon what color suited the sisters at the time.

# Chapter Three

When one wanted to take a bath, large buckets of water heated on the big black iron stove in the kitchen were poured into a hat tub by a manservant, who had placed the tub in one's bedroom in front of the fireplace, which appeared to be the proper place for a hat tub to stand, even in summer when one did not need the heat of the fire. On one side of its wide flaring brim was a seat for the bather and a holder for soap, and when I was a child, bathing in a hat tub was a far more enjoyable experience than bathing in the sort of bathtubs we had in town.

Although, to Aunt Matilda's great disappointment she could not have a bathroom like those in town, the sisters rejoiced in having a telephone and mail service. The postman came twice a week, riding a horse with his saddlebags bulging with mail, and he visited homes that were within a certain radius of town.

As time went by, the state delayed in establishing the promised Rural Electrification System, so Aunt Matilda became impatient and decided to invent a bathroom built according to her own design. She had a room added to the back of the house and a second well dug just down the hill, above which was erected a tall windmill of steel that had large propellers resembling those on the windmills in Holland.

The propellers were designed to depend upon the mingled breezes from the mountains, the river, and the creek to draw water through pipes laid underground from the newly dug well to the newly built bathroom. When the breezes blew, the propellers whirled at a lively rate and water rushed through the pipes, but when the breezes failed, as they often did, the propellers turned slowly, creaking mournfully, and not a drop of water was to be had.

Consequently, when I was visiting at Bellevue and waked on summer mornings, this melancholy sound, made by the slow moving propellers, was what I usually heard, along with the dull thudding of the big wooden water bucket that was banded in brass bumping against the interior of the well at the back door, and with the creaking of the windlass, as a servant drew fresh water for breakfast.

However, the delicious breakfast smells that hung upon the air were enough to bring me quickly from my bed to meet the morning—a morning that seemed to sparkle and glisten like none other on earth. The sun touched the hilltop and the house upon it before its rays reached down into the bottom lands, and every leaf and blade of grass upon the hilltop seemed to catch its light. During the night diligent spiders had spun webs in the big green boxwood bushes which held drops of dew that winked and sparkled like diamonds. Dewdrop diamonds also lay scattered across the lawn and it was a joy for a child to run barefoot through the shining, icy, dew drenched grass.

It was also a surprise at times to see that, although the hilltop was illumined by the sun, the bottom lands were often covered by an opaque, silver-white ocean of fog, out of which the hilltop seemed to rise like some magically gilded island in a dream.

Breakfast was always bountiful, for the practical Aunt Matilda said that an army marches on its stomach and that we, too, needed a substantial repast with which to begin the day. At first I found this statement puzzling, for it was difficult to imagine an army advancing, worm-like upon its stomachs—to say nothing of such dignified ladies as Aunt Mary Lou and Aunt Matilda—but discernment came with time.

When Aunt Matilda told Aunt Mary Lou she was too thin and urged her to eat more, Aunt Mary Lou always replied in her old-fashioned way that she had "a gracious plenty and anything more would be a satiety." She also said that eating too much was "an imposition upon the stomach" and after supper peppermint candies (called peppermint drops) were served because the ladies agreed that they were "an aid to the digestive process."

When visiting my aunts I always slept with Aunt Mary Lou in a large double sleigh bed upstairs. The big carved walnut bed the sisters shared in a downstairs bedroom had a feather tick upon it filled with goose feathers that became a second mattress and was as delightfully soft and comfortable as the fleeciest summer cloud appeared to be. It could easily have accommodated the three of us, but Aunt Matilda, probably because of the "inflammatory rheumatism" in her knees, did not relish the idea of spending the night with a possibly restless small child. Because of this, Aunt Mary Lou always took me to "the girls' room," the big square bedroom over the parlor where she and several of her sisters had slept when they were young, and she always went like a homing pigeon to the old-fashioned sleigh bed she and Aunt Matilda had once shared.

Before going to bed, the three of us undressed in their bedroom downstairs, and, when ready for bed, the sisters reminded me of bishops of the Episcopal Church. Both wore voluminous white cambric nightgowns that reached the floor, which were gathered onto yokes, with long, full sleeves with ruffles at the wrists. They made

## Chapter Three

Aunt Mary Lou look like a bishop who was tall and thin and Aunt Matilda like one who was short and plump. They also wore night caps, tied with ribbons under the chin. Aunt Matilda's night caps and gowns had embroidery and lace, but Aunt Mary Lou's were plain.

Under their nightgowns each lady wore a chemise (sometimes referred to as a shimmy), which was a full shirt-like garment without sleeves that was made of the sheerest white cotton batiste and reached to the knees. A garment of this type was also worn by ladies of their generation under their clothing in the daytime, for it went without saying that no lady would ever dream of being caught, dead or alive, without her chemise.

When fully arrayed for bed, we knelt and said our prayers, but Aunt Matilda's and mine were not as long as Aunt Mary Lou's, so when Aunt Matilda had finished praying she climbed into bed upon the big soft featherbed and invited me to share it with her until Aunt Mary Lou was through.

Sometimes we both fell asleep and I remember being suddenly jolted awake one night by hearing Aunt Matilda, who had also fallen asleep and then awakened, calling out to Aunt Mary Lou.

"Get up, Mary Lou! Get up off your knees!" she ordered. "You'll catch your death of cold kneeling there in the night breeze with nothing on but your gown and chemise—and, anyway, you've already told the Lord enough!"

Aunt Mary Lou rose from her knees, picked up a lamp, and I followed her upstairs to "the girls' room." The sleigh bed had a featherbed upon it too, and across the head of the bed was a long sausage-shaped pillow called a bolster. Atop the bolster sat two fat pillows, that, like the bolster, were filled with goose feathers.

The bolster and pillows had white linen cases with embroidered scallops, and I was intrigued by the fact that on one pillow case was embroidered, "I slept and dreamed that life was beauty," and on the other, "I woke and found that life was duty."

Across the foot of the bed there was folded a friendship quilt, because nights on the hilltop often grew cool, even in the warmest weather. Friendship quilts were products of the poverty stricken days during the Reconstruction Period after the Civil War when ladies swapped quilting scraps of worn out dresses to make these much needed bed coverlets. Many were made from scraps of party frocks, ball gowns, and other fine dresses; so the quilts, being of silk, velvet, satin, taffeta, or brocade were often beautiful as well as useful. Adding a poignant sentimentality to the varicolored pieces were the names of the donors of the scraps, who often embroidered their names upon them as well as the dates at which they were given.

One summer night just after the sisters and I had finished our prayers downstairs and were ready for bed, we were startled by the squawking of chickens that seemed to come from the direction of the big hemlock tree down by the front gate, and, at this, both ladies paused.

"Somebody's after my chickens!" Aunt Matilda announced.

For some reason known only to the chicken mind, these annoying fowls had a liking for roosting at night in that particular tree; so whenever a few could escape from the poultry lot, they scooted right down to the front gate, flew up into the hemlock and spent the night—which never failed to annoy Aunt Matilda.

"Maybe it's just an owl that has scared the chickens because it wants to roost there, too." Aunt Mary Lou suggested, remembering this had happened in the past.

"No. They're making a different sort of racket!" Aunt Matilda said, reaching into her top bureau drawer and lifting out her little pistol that had a handle of mother-of-pearl, which she kept hidden under a stack of embroidered and lace-edged handkerchiefs.

At the sight, Aunt Mary Lou recoiled. "Put down that gun, Matilda!"

"I'll do nothing of the sort! It's a chicken thief and I'm not going to let him get away with it!"

Aunt Mary Lou clasped her hands in front of her as though in prayer. "If it really is a man, can't you just give him a good talking-to?"

"Oh for goodness sakes, Mary Lou!"

Aunt Matilda laid the pistol aside while she hastily got into her robe, and Aunt Mary Lou automatically followed suit, knowing that when Aunt Matilda started something and looked so determined she was going to follow through on whatever she had in mind. She started to speak again, but Aunt Matilda cut her off by picking up the pistol and shouting for Estelle, her adoring black maid of many long years, who had already gone to bed but came bounding up the back hall, pop-eyed with fright.

"Pick up the lamp, Estelle," Aunt Matilda ordered. "I can't carry it and shoot, too."

Estelle took up the lamp with a trembling hand and followed her mistress to the front door and then onto the front porch, while Aunt

Mary Lou and I followed fearfully in the rear. Then in the pool of yellow lamplight on the porch, Aunt Matilda took her stand and aimed the pistol toward the front gate.

"If there's a man up in that tree by the gate, let him speak—or I'll shoot!" she called.

Her clear ringing tones echoed through the night, but no man answered. The chickens continued to squawk and Aunt Mary Lou, growing desperate, tried again.

"Remember the Ten Commandments, Matilda! Thou shalt not kill!"

"Hush up, Mary Lou!" Aunt Matilda descended the steps to the front walk, ordering, "Estelle, hold the lamp a little higher—so I can see better to shoot."

Aunt Mary Lou wrung her hands in desperation. "Please, Matilda—if it is a man—please just try to shoot at the legs!"

"I'll do no such thing!" Aunt Matilda spoke loudly enough to be heard easily down by the gate. "If I have to shoot, I'll shoot to kill!"

"No, ma'am! No, ma'am!" a frightened voice yelled from the hemlock tree. There was a commotion amongst its branches. A shadowy figure dropped to the ground, and Sam, a black handyman on the place, hurried up the front walk into the circle of lamplight, holding a large, fat opossum by the tail, so that it hung upside down. "Them chickens was just fussin' at this here ole possum. He been ramblin' round here a day or so—and when I heard them chickens I figgered it was him and clumb up to see."

"What are you going to do with it?" I asked, very much interested since it was the first opossum I had ever seen.

"Eat him. That's what. Possum's mighty tasty wid sweet taters cooked in the pot." Noting my interest, he added, "Hold out yo' finger, lil Missy."

Foolishly I obeyed, at which he caught hold of the animal's tail closer to its body freeing the end, which wrapped itself so quickly and tightly about my finger that I screamed in fright while the others laughed.

Although the chickens and the opossum in the hemlock tree caused a good deal of excitement, that was the only time I was ever frightened while visiting my aunts. However, I learned there was another event that occurred before I was born when two of my cousins, boys of about nine or ten years old, were visiting at Bellevue, and the courageous Aunt Matilda even became frightened.

It took place on a summer night after the sisters, their young visitors and Estelle had already gone to bed and were asleep. Then the frightening yells and shouts of a nocturnal intruder rang out. The culprit turned out to be the wife of one of the black tenants on the place—she had gone berserk and had begun pounding on the front door with a large stick.

She also started shouting, "I'm gonna set the world on fire and go up in the smoke! I'm gonna set the world on fire and go up in the smoke!"

At this, everyone rolled hastily out of bed and the sisters put on their robes. Aunt Matilda, as usual, took charge. A procession formed and wended its way to the front door, with Aunt Matilda in front. Estelle carried the lamp close behind her, and Aunt Mary Lou and the boys followed in the rear.

Aunt Matilda ordered the unwelcome guest to stop shouting and pounding with the stick and to make herself known, but her order was ignored. The pounding and shouting continued, and, since setting the world on fire would naturally include the house and its environs, Aunt Mary Lou was emboldened to speak.

"Matilda, the poor soul must be demented," she said. "Perhaps we should open the door, speak to her kindly and find out what is the matter."

"The idea of such a thing! You're the one who must be demented!" Aunt Matilda shot back.

Aunt Mary Lou winced at the heavy blows of the stick upon the door. She took a step forward, adding, "I'll just open the door a crack and speak to the poor creature."

Aunt Matilda blocked her way. "If you dare touch that door, Mary Lou, I'll . . . I'll . . . " She hastily searched her mind for a threat dire enough to stop her sister in her tracks. "I'll . . . I'll . . . I'll slap you, Mary Lou. And I'll slap you hard!"

Her eye fell upon the two boys quaking with fright at her side and she ordered, "You boys will have to run for help!" She rushed them to the back door, gave them the name of a brawny tenant who did not live far away, and pushed them out of the back door, commanding, "Run to get him as fast as you can!"

At the next moment they were off and running like rabbits, but to her dismay, the pounding on the front door and the shouting stopped abruptly. Footsteps thudded across the front porch and down the steps, which could only mean that the intruder had gotten wind of what was going on and was taking off around the side of the house after the boys, which was confirmed a few moments later by their yells of terror.

Ignoring her own safety, Aunt Matilda grabbed up her megaphone, which she used for summoning tenants working in the fields when she needed to talk with them. She hurried onto the back porch as fast as she could, and trumpeted through the night the news of what was taking place at the house on the hill, at the same time urging all courageous men who were strong of limb and within hearing of her voice to come to her aid at once.

Aunt Mary Lou also sprang into action. She dashed to the telephone that hung in the back hall, cranked it up as rapidly as she was able, and ordered Maybelle to inform the county sheriff as to what was taking place and to urge him to come immediately. At this, the excitable and greatly interested Maybelle rang up the sheriff, and in her agitation began ringing telephones willy-nilly all up and down the valley, to spread the news and ask for help.

Due to Maybelle and the stentorian tones of Aunt Matilda through the megaphone, which had carried farther than she knew through the stilly night, it was not long before the sheriff and his posse arrived, armed and ready for conflict.

Along with them came every male tenant on the place, also ready for conflict, and shortly afterwards there arrived a large number of persons upon whom the sisters had never set eyes before. Some came on foot, some on horseback and muleback. Others came in buggies, wagons, and carts, and many brought along their wives and children, all having risen hastily from their beds and set forth in the night—not wishing, they said, "to miss out on anything."

It was not long before the sheriff and his men had corralled the cause of so much alarm and taken her off to the hospital in Morganton. The two boys were found, terrified but unharmed, in the barn, where they had fled to hide when the intruder chased them.

After calm was restored, the only thing that was left to be done was to telephone Maybelle, who was eagerly waiting to learn the full story of all that had taken place. This Aunt Matilda related to her, but it was not until the sky grew pink with dawn before everyone in the house went to bed and fell into an exhausted sleep.

The only other scare at Bellevue that I was told about also took place many years before I was born, and it did not occur at night but on a bright, sunny morning in the fall when a brisk autumn wind was blowing. At the time Aunt Mary Lou happened to be upstairs in the "girls' room" over the parlor and she was terrified by the yells and screams of the servants and the shouts of , "Fire! Fire! The kitchen's on fire!"

The kitchen, like all country kitchens of that day, stood nearby but to the rear of the home, and as she listened to the bedlam and saw smoke and cinders flying skyward outside the back bedroom windows, she was galvanized by fright, feeling certain that the wooden shingles on the roof of the house would catch fire at any moment and the house itself would go up in flames. Then she realized that she should save something of value before this occurred, and the moment this idea popped into her mind, she went to work.

Nearby stood a bureau in which Aunt Matilda kept her best and fanciest lingerie, upon which she set great store, along with packets of love letters tied with ribbons that she had treasured through the years. Hastily opening the bureau drawers, Aunt Mary Lou scooped up their contents and flung them out a front window, not realizing that as she quickly cast them out, the wind just as quickly swept most of them up into the branches of the two tall cedar trees in front of the house.

The kitchen, which was two stories high, had four rooms, the two below serving as a cooking room and a storage room and the two above providing quarters for Aunt Dicie, the cook. The entire building burned to the ground, but the house was miraculously unharmed.

When at last a measure of calm was restored, Aunt Matilda went out onto the front porch to sit down and rest for a few moments while she tried to get hold of herself. Then she sustained an even greater shock on seeing the two big cedars in front of the house decorated like Christmas trees with her most intimate and personal belongings.

Clinging to branches, both high and low, were chemises, corsets, corset covers, flounced petticoats, stockings, lacy negligees, handkerchiefs, drawers with ribbons and lace edging, silk scarves of various colors, and other feminine furbelows that were dear to her heart—not to mention the love letters, that, loosed from their ribbons, fluttered and danced about on the front lawn, tossed playfully by the wind in and out of bushes along the way.

When she could get herself together, she summoned all boys on the place, both black and white, and soon they were climbing, monkey-like, amongst the branches of the cedar trees. Some garments could be retrieved, but others hung so high that they could not be dislodged even after efforts were made to pry them loose with hoes, potato diggers, and extra long fishing poles, and on these she had to

# Chapter Three

wait several months until a heavy rain and the strong winds of winter swept them down.

There were only two garments that defied all efforts to bring them to earth. One was the fanciest be-ribboned and lacy pair of drawers that Aunt Matilda possessed, and the other a sheer lace-edged chemise. Sometimes, to Aunt Matilda's relief, the drawers wrapped themselves modestly about the small but sturdy limb to which they clung, but at other times, at a sudden blast of wind, they sprang forth in all their shameless splendor for the world to see—until one day during a storm they dropped to the lawn, a sodden rain drenched mass, fit only to be thrown away.

The chemise held out much longer, impaled upon a twig at the outmost tip of a bough. There was something ghostlike about it, Aunt Matilda said, for on moonlit nights it could be seen filmy white, almost transparent, moving rhythmically to and fro; or air-filled, dancing about in the wind like a balloon. As the winter wore on she kept a despairing eye upon it, deciding it would float there forever, unaffected by wind or rain. Then, to her surprise and relief, it departed one night while she was asleep and went upon its mysterious way.

Where had it gone? I wondered when I heard the story. In my imagination I could see it sailing higher and still higher in the moonlight, in sight for a moment and then disappearing—until morning came and the sunlight took it, making it shimmer with a pale unearthly tint.

"Do you guess it's still sailing on?" I asked.

"Who knows?" answered Aunt Matilda.

Maybe, she said, it had sailed on to China or some other outlandish place and she really didn't care, so long as it had sailed off the cedar tree. What she continued to worry about were the love letters that had blown far and wide across the fields and meadows. Some of them had taken to the air like kites and there was no way of telling where they had landed.

It made her cringe to think about their being read by strangers up and down the valley, and especially by people she knew in town. Some had been written by prominent gentlemen in the community who, smitten by her charms when they were young, had asked her to marry them before they had even courted their wives, who were Aunt Matilda's close friends. What if those gentlemen, who had become dignified husbands and fathers of numerous offspring, should happen to read the ridiculous love-sick lines they had once penned, and what of their wives?

One love letter was picked up in the vegetable garden by Estelle, and Aunt Matilda received it with great relief. It had been written by a staid and pompous old gentleman in town, the father of many offspring, whom I knew when he had become elderly, and in whose bosom I would never have thought such a passion of love could have ever germinated, even in his youthful years.

"I love you as man never loved woman—nor will ever love again," he had written. "You are as fair as Mother Eve, fresh from the hands of her Maker."

Aunt Mary Lou and I could not help bursting into laughter at these impassioned words, and in our laughter the relieved Aunt Matilda joined, along with Estelle, who had been trying to comfort her.

"Just put all them love letters outer yo' mind, Miss Matilda—and that shimmy what hung on that tree so long. I bet it just blowed up the river no farther than Willow Tree Church and then mebbe just got hung up in one of them willow trees round the baptizin' hole."

"Gracious! I hope not," said Aunt Matilda.

Estelle pondered a moment and had a new thought. "Well, if it skeers the chillun, mebbe thinkin' it be a ghost up in them trees—or if the Reverend Bascomb git the notion it might be some sort of sign from the Lord—why, I'll just tell him it ain't nothin' but Miss Matilda's shimmy what blowed up the river."

"No! No! The least said the better. Pray, say nothing!" begged Aunt Matilda.

When she became older, Aunt Matilda could laugh about this unfortunate episode, but I felt she still had a slight feeling of embarrassment even though it had happened so long ago. After all, she said, there were people still living in the town and valley who had heard about or had even seen her most intimate garments decorating the cedar trees.

As for the love letters, there were certainly some persons still alive who had found and read them, and were laughing about them behind her back; and she confessed that for years after the unfortunate episode she had winced at the thought of it.

Because of the rheumatism in her knees, Aunt Matilda found it difficult to climb up into and down out of buggies, since they were swung so high off the ground. They were built this way to enable them to travel unpaved country roads that were sometimes deep in mud, to cross over brooks and small streams, and, even, to ford rivers when necessary. She had complained about this for some time, but being the enterprising and determined person that she was, she had finally decided to do something about the problem.

To our astonishment, we found that, although she had failed in creating a bathroom like those in town, she was a genius at designing a buggy. She said she had come up with a design in her mind that suited her in every way and it would be "custom built" with all the conveniences and gadgets for comfort that she had always desired.

It arrived by train in a boxcar and I was filled with admiration at the sight of it, for it was the most elegant buggy I had ever set eyes upon. It was not only swung much closer to the ground than other buggies, but it had a dashboard that curved forward and then back as gracefully as the breast of a swan. Its seat was comfortably cushioned in tufted black leather and was wide enough for three persons instead of only two. Its top projected so far forward that passengers were protected from the weather, even during a rain; for then a curtain of imitation black leather could be hung up in front, attached by snaps to the dashboard and the projecting top.

In the center of this curtain was a large window of almost transparent isinglass and beside it were slits for the reins and the buggy whip. There was also a smaller window of isinglass above the seat in the back because Aunt Matilda liked to see what was following behind as well as what was coming along in front.

Another important asset was that it had fat rubber tires and heavy coiled springs that cushioned the ride on even the most deeply rutted roads. Being swung so low it could not ford the river, but Aunt Matilda did not wish it to do so because a bridge had been built a mile upstream above the river ford. It was promptly named the Low Buggy, whereas after this, the other buggy on the place was called the High Buggy and Aunt Matilda never set foot in the High Buggy again.

The animal that drew this elegant buggy was worthy of this distinction. A big bay named Clock because of the rhythmic, clock-like precision of his trot, he had a satiny, well curried coat and wore a silver mounted bridle and harness (relics of a more prosperous day before the Civil War), and when he felt Aunt Matilda's plump, firm hands upon the reins he gave a stellar performance.

Aside from all this, Aunt Matilda, who took to buggy driving like a bee to clover, saw an extra advantage in the Low Buggy. It would not only enable her to go to town in more comfort and style, but she could visit her old friends who lived here and there about the valley more often and more easily than in the past. She set about making these calls at once, and since they often took place while I was visiting the ladies, I went along, too.

Ensconced in the tufted black leather interior of the Low Buggy, riding comfortably upon its coiled springs and rubber tired wheels, she, Aunt Mary Lou and I followed winding country roads, crossed brooks and shallow streams, penetrated thick woodlands and passed through widespread meadows dotted with white and gold daisies, blue ragged robins, and misty white Queen Anne's lace.

One of the old homes my aunts enjoyed visiting was about six miles up the valley and in reaching it we had to pass through two small crossroad communities. One was called Worry and the other Joy, and I was intrigued by the fact that we had to go through Worry to get to Joy.

In the home we visited, there lived three elderly ladies—Miss Susie, Miss Emmie and Miss Lizzie, but all of them were not maiden ladies. Miss Emmie was a widow and Miss Lizzie had a perfectly good husband whom we children liked and called Mr. Bob. Since we always saw him and the sisters in a bunch, however, it was hard to remember to which one he belonged.

Many of the old homes we visited had names that I can never forget—among them Brookwood, Creekside, Ash Hill, Swan Ponds, Quaker Meadows, Maplewood, Willow Hill, Cedar Grove, Belvedere, Magnolia, and Pleasant Gardens. In their high-ceilinged old rooms we found furnishings very much like those at Bellevue: imported matching mantel vases with flowers or castles or pastoral scenes painted on them; big flat topped pianos with keys made of ivory with places for candles and lamps at each end of the keyboards; sofas upholstered with well worn velvet or horsehair; and portraits of ancestors that watched silently from the walls.

Refreshments were always served, as at Bellevue, and at the homes that were too far from town to be visited by the Ice Wagon, there were ice ponds. Consequently, the ice that tinkled pleasantly in the cut glass tumblers of lemonade or tea was apt to have a pebble or two in it or, even, a few blades of grass—which made the drink all the more interesting to a child. Incidentally, the springhouses at these old homes were usually built of brick and stood astride the spot where a clear ice cold spring of water bubbled from the earth. Inside the buildings were shelves along the walls to hold foods that needed to be kept chilled, and the water that rushed through the center of the building and ran out under the door became on the outside an ice-cold brook in which a child delighted to wade.

When I was small I sometimes felt sorry for Miss Susie because she had never caught a husband, but I found later on, due to a statement she once made to me, that she was both satisfied with and proud of her station in life.

"My dear, she said, "I am a most fortunate woman. I am the daughter of a Southern gentleman who was an elder in the Presbyterian Church and an officer in the Confederate Army. Who could wish for more?"

My aunts enjoyed these visits to the three sisters greatly and so did I —and also the cookies and the generous slices of delicious layer cakes that were served with the lemonade or tea. They continued these visits for many months—until an unexpected and terrifying catastrophe occurred, that for quite a while, put a stop to the rides in the low buggy and the high buggy, too.

*Two Ladies Marooned in a Flood — Civil War Tales —
The Wedding Dress in the Parlor Chimney — The
Christmas Log — Starvation Parties*

### 4.

When it began to rain that summer of 1916 no one dreamed that it would continue to pour for days and that we were going to have the worst flood that the western part of North Carolina had ever known. The town of Morganton stood on high ground, so was not thought to be in danger, but as the rivers and creeks began to overflow their banks and rush into the bottom lands, many persons in the valley began to leave their homes and seek refuge in town.

We begged Aunt Mary Lou and Aunt Matilda to leave home and come to stay with us, but they refused to budge from the big brick house on the hill. We knew, of course, that the ladies, each in her own way, were keeping an eye on the steadily rising waters. The practical Aunt Matilda told us she had sent the tenants living in the lowlands to safer quarters on higher ground and had "laid in plentiful supplies," and we knew without being told that the prayerful Aunt Mary Lou was continually praying for the rain to stop.

This does not mean that Aunt Matilda was not prayerful, too. Like her sister, she prayed daily and was determined to be on hand and numbered with the elect when the role is called up yonder. It was just that she believed that, while continuing in prayer, it did no harm to keep an eye peeled for unexpected emergencies. Thus, having battened down the hatches, as the saying goes, she had decided, along with Aunt Mary Lou, that they would ride out the flood in the house on the hill just like Noah in the Ark.

As the days passed, the rain continued and the waters rose still higher. We knew that the ladies would soon be marooned on the hilltop with no chance of escape, but they reminded us that the hill upon which the house stood was not just a hill. It was really a peninsula jutting out into the lowlands from a high wooded area that could be used for an escape even if the hill should be completely surrounded by water on its other three sides. They told us this by telephone, which had become our only means of communication with the sisters after the waters began to cover all roads to town.

"The time has come to leave the place!" my father told Aunt Matilda, shouting in order to be heard over the noises that were steadily growing louder and more raucous on the telephone line.

"Oh, I'm sure we'll be all right!" Aunt Matilda yelled back cheerfully. "So do stop worrying!"

"Do as I say! Leave the house at once!" he shouted. "Use the old closed carriage and get one of the younger men on the place to drive you out. Go up through the woods and follow one of the old logging trails and head towards the mountains. Soon all roads to town will be deep under water—so, whatever you do, don't come this way!"

Although the old closed carriage had not been used in a long time, it was in good condition the last time it was driven, and so far as we knew, it was still the best vehicle on the place to be used in a downpour.

"Will you please stop worrying!" Aunt Matilda shouted over the telephone the next morning. "We've been through floods before and the water has never come up as high as the boxwoods at the lower end of the lawn. I'm sure it won't this time either!"

That afternoon Aunt Mary Lou telephoned to say, through the noises that were getting steadily louder on the telephone line, that the water was beginning to creep up towards the barn, which stood below and at some distance from the house. She and Aunt Matilda were still not alarmed, but the next morning she called to report that the water was still rising and had come up to the barn.

"Since you are so worried," Aunt Matilda broke in, "if the water comes up the hill as high as the boxwoods at the end of the front lawn, we'll get out. Stop worrying. I can manage."

Shortly after this, the telephone emitted a long mournful wail and then went dead, indicating that the telephone poles that marched across the valley were being buffeted so strongly by the surging waters that they had gone down, dragging the lines with them, and future communication would be impossible. Then, being too worried about the ladies to remain at home, we began going to the high bluff just outside town that overlooked the valley, and there we always found a crowd of townsfolk, huddled under umbrellas in the downpour, watching the mud colored ocean that stretched in every direction, so far as we could see.

Poking up here and there out of the water were small grassy or wooded islands that were really the tops of hills, and borne upon the swift and treacherous torrent was debris that told a grisly story: parts of roofs torn from houses and barns; fences and posts; uprooted trees; and worst of all, dead animals—horses, mules, cows, pigs, and sheep.

We peered continually in the direction of Bellevue, which was too far away to be seen, and wondered if the water had risen as high as the boxwood bushes, at which time the aunts had agreed to leave home. Had they actually left and were they following some mountain road that was deep in mud, seeking shelter wherever they could find it? Regardless of their plight, we felt certain it would be some time before we saw them and we prayed that when we did, they would be alive and unharmed.

The next day about noon my father was told that the crowd on the bluff outside town was witnessing a blood-chilling drama. Out in the vast muddy sea a small portion of the roof of a submerged brick building could be seen and upon it there was a man; he was leaping about and gesticulating wildly to attract attention and get someone to save him. Later we were to learn that when the water began to rise, his family had left in a canoe, but he, not thinking the flood would be so catastrophic, had remained behind. When the waters rose to the first floor of the building he had climbed to the second floor and when this became flooded, too, he had ascended to the roof. My father was told that if he were not rescued shortly he would certainly drown, but no one could be found who would attempt such a dangerous undertaking. Then the question was put: Would my father go?

In his college days my father had been a fine athlete and he was still a strong and vigorous man for his age, but he was nearly fifty years old at the time. When he agreed to go, my mother was panic stricken and she grew still more upset when her father, who happened to be visiting us and was in his seventies, said at once to my father, "I'll go with you."

My father hurried out to his automobile that stood in the driveway in front of the house, ready at all times for our trips to view the flood. My grandfather and mother followed him and I, taking advantage of the situation, scrambled unnoticed into the back seat. When we reached the bluff, where, as usual, a crowd had gathered, my father sprang out of the automobile, my grandfather close behind him. They started down the steep muddy bank to the water, but at that moment, we saw a boat manned by two much younger men pulling off from shore.

Fortunately the roof upon which the endangered man waited was downstream, so after much tugging and straining at the oars, the two oarsmen were able to bring the boat close enough to help him into it; and at the next moment they were swept out of sight. We feared we might never see any of them again, but the next day we heard that they all had landed safely several miles below town.

A few minutes after they had disappeared we became aware of a stirring in the crowd of onlookers upon the bluff. Heads were turned. Necks were stretched. Then in the watery distance we glimpsed two strange looking objects coming downstream, swept swiftly toward us by the current. As we watched, they drew nearer and took form, becoming two boats, one following the other—two flat-bottomed bateaux of the sort used for hauling on the rivers and creeks—and in each of them two oarsmen, fore and aft, struggled to keep them on course, seeming almost unable to do so.

Then to our amazement, we saw that in the first boat sat Aunt Matilda under a big black umbrella, her luggage about her feet. As she drew still nearer, we saw that she was dressed as for an important occasion, which indeed it was. Her bonnet was set at its most becoming angle on her carefully waved silver hair and on her face was a look of triumph and delight as she viewed the astonished throng waiting in the downpour on top of the bluff.

In the boat behind her sat Aunt Mary Lou under a big black umbrella, her luggage at her feet. She was dressed as usual in somber black and on her face was a look that can be described as being compounded of confidence in the power of prayer and thanksgiving for the mercy and protection of the Lord.

The oarsmen had difficulty in bringing the two boats to land and it was the retiring Aunt Mary Lou who stepped ashore first—the only time I ever knew her to precede her more ebullient and aggressive sister. In a few minutes Aunt Matilda joined her on the muddy bank, looking like Queen Victoria ready to receive her court, and at this there was cheering from the crowd on the bluff—which she acknowledged with a queenly tilt of her head. She had managed, just as she said she would.

Soon the ladies were comfortably settled at our house in town and it was there they had to stay for several months, for the flood had left much devastation in its wake. The roads in the valley had been almost destroyed and the sisters could not go home until they could at least be made passable. I was seven years old at the time and in school, and like all Southern children of my age, I was greatly interested in stories about the Civil War. Of course, I had already heard a lot of them, but I still wanted to hear all my aunts could tell; so with the two staying in our home for such a long time, I took advantage of the situation to hear still more.

"Were you really very poor after the Civil War?" I asked Aunt Mary Lou.

"Yes, child we were," she said. "All the South was poor, but somehow with the grace of the Lord, we managed to get along."

It was easy to see that both sisters enjoyed a steaming cup of breakfast coffee with sugar and cream, and Aunt Matilda remarked on how much better real coffee tasted than the so-called coffee they had to drink during and after the war, which was made of parched corn or wheat and sweetened with a little molasses or sweet potatoes, although these additions did not improve the flavor. She also said that during and after the war they missed having sugar, especially at Christmas time, to make candy and cakes for the younger brothers and sisters. Having to go without, they searched the woods for walnuts, hickory nuts, and chestnuts to put in the children's stockings and they always managed to find a nice apple in the orchard to put in the toe of each.

All the Christmas gifts for the family had to be homemade, so there were rag dolls stuffed with cotton with cheeks painted pink with pokeberry juice, hair painted red and yellow with the juice of sumac found in the woods, and eyes painted with indigo or walnut hull dye.

At boarding school, the artistic Aunt Mary Lou had studied art, so when her oil paints gave out they searched the woods for substitute colors and she said she "tried to paint a happy look on every doll's face because the times were so sad and hard." Other gifts on those long ago Christmases were doll beds and toy wagons made of cornstalks, the latter with spools for wheels; small toy animals whittled out of wood by an old servant on the place; and flutes made of river reeds from which the pith had been pushed out with a heated wire.

Sometimes the better parts of worn out dresses were sewn together to make a "new" dress, and since the pieces were of different colors, Aunt Dicie, the cook at Bellevue, became an expert at dyeing in an effort to make these dresses of one color instead of a patchwork of different hues. In the happier days before the war, Aunt Dicie had possessed, along with her skill in cooking, a certain literary flair. Once when Margaret, one of the little sisters at Bellevue, was engaged in writing a poem about music, she read what she had written to the old woman and requested her aid in enumerating all the things in which music could be found.

"Lawsee me! I can write a better pome than that!" Aunt Dicie exclaimed.

Then she gave utterance to the following lines, which the delighted little girl wrote down:

> *There's music in the pots,*
> *There's music in the kittles,*
> *There's music in the knife and fork*
> *What cut's up the vittles.*

Aunt Dicie put away her literary gifts, however, in the emergency. Her genius in dyeing garments was put to the fore, and upon this the sisters had to rely. They tried to be thankful for what they had—that is, all except Aunt Matilda, who had set her heart on possessing a crimson silk dancing frock—crimson being just the color to set off her white skin and sparkling dark eyes—but which her sisters thought would be as hard to come by as the moon.

At this point, their mother came to the rescue by getting out her wedding dress of white silk with an overdress of heavy white lace, both imported from Paris. She had tied the dress in a sheet with her husband's brocaded wedding vest and some jewelry and hidden them in the parlor chimney which kept them safe from Bloody Kirk, the mountain raiders, and the Yankee soldiers.

The white lace she gave to Aunt Mary Lou, who wore it over an old white dress, and Aunt Mary Lou said the dress she concocted "really made a very nice showing." The underdress of white silk, which she gave to Aunt Matilda, she put in the care of Aunt Dicie, who gathered pokeberries from the thickets along the creek and river. Then she plunged the dress into a big pot of boiling pokeberry juice with a few rusty nails in the bottom of the pot to "set the dye." The pleased Aunt Matilda wore it over a tilterine, the widest hoop skirt of the day, and had her hair done up in a "waterfall"—that is, brushed to the top of her head, with curls cascading down to her shoulders—a most becoming arrangement. Thus arrayed, each sister, wearing her portion of the wedding dress, went about to social affairs after the war that were called "starvation parties" because no refreshments were served, due to the scarcity of food, which had to be carefully hoarded.

"We tried our best to have a good time in spite of it," the social and gregarious Aunt Matilda said, "And later on, after times grew better, we were able to have a little molasses cake and sometimes a small glass of homemade apple cider."

"Things were very different then from the way they had been before the war," Aunt Mary Lou added.

"Oh, so different!" Aunt Matilda agreed. "Before the war there was plenty for all. We danced and feasted—the blacks as well as the whites. The black people always cut down a tree to make a large Yule Log a good while before Christmas. It was cut to fit the big fireplace in the parlor. They soaked it in the creek, so that it would take a long while to burn, and while it burned all the black people had a holiday and did no work. That included the house servants, too. They did only the minimum of work that was necessary to keep the house running."

"But we all, black and white, went to church on Christmas Day," Aunt Mary Lou added. "For Pa and Mother wanted everyone to remember that it was the birthday of our Lord Jesus Christ."

After my aunts returned home following the flood, the person to whom I went for stories of the Civil War was beautiful Aunt Claudia, who lived just down our street. She, too, had been a girl during the war and she had many memories about those hard long ago Christmases, so she could tell stories that supplemented those of Aunt Mary Lou and Aunt Matilda. As for the presents that were given, she said, pins and needles were popular gifts because they could not be obtained. If any could be found about the house they were pinned on brightly colored slips of paper and used for gifts for the ladies and girls, who were delighted to have them.

Homemade pin cushions were also popular gifts. They were stuffed with cotton and made out of silk and velvet scraps from worn-out party dresses. There were also spools of thread that were really the ravellings of worn-out silk dresses or silk scarves. For the gentlemen, there were pen wipers made of velvet or woolen scraps, and, since there was no shoe polish to be had, there were little bottles and jars of polish made of lard blackened with soot that was scraped from the inside of chimneys.

Ink was not obtainable, so they saved what ink they had and added water to it, which made it so pale that the words could scarcely be read. Writing paper could not be had, so they gave little packets of paper that were made of wallpaper they had soaked with a wet rag and then, after cutting it in squares with a sharp knife, peeled from the walls. In time they discovered that pokeberry juice made better ink, so they put it into little bottles, and it was sometimes used in its natural red color and sometimes darkened with soot. Since there was no sealing wax to seal the letters, peach tree resin was gathered in the orchard, heated to the right consistency and rolled into little balls that could be used to seal letters in place of sealing wax. Letters were written only when it was necessary to inform relatives and close friends of important matters, and a space was left at the bottom of the paper for a reply, since it went without saying that the person who received the letter was without writing paper, too.

These wallpaper letters, written with pokeberry juice and sealed with peach resin, went back and forth in the mails many times and when there was no space left for writing, they were turned sideways and additional letters were written criss-cross upon them.

When the soles of shoes wore out, new soles were made of wood and the upper parts were fashioned of cloth. Blankets were often dyed and made into heavy shawls that were worn instead of cloaks by both ladies and gentlemen. Aunt Claudia told me that in the deeper South hats were woven of broomstraw for both sexes, and hickory nut shells with holes bored in them to hold the thread were used for buttons. But, worst of all, she said, the Confederate money was worthless, and could buy nothing at all.

"So you can imagine what a hard time we had," she added. "But in the deeper South, where the devastation was still greater, it was even worse."

Aunt Claudia, to my delight, was also a good teller of Civil War tales—although not quite so good as Aunt Mary Lou, who had a real gift for story telling and a way of making the people in her stories appear to actually come alive. There was one story, however, that I found most amusing and asked her to tell it a number of times. It was about my father's uncle, John Holt, a tall, dignified and impressive old gentleman who was a pillar of the Episcopal Church in the nearby town in which he lived.

Uncle John owned a large dog of a breed called a mastiff, which was popular in the old gentleman's time. In that day, dogs were allowed to go to church with their owners, being taught not to bark but to lie quietly under the church pew upon which their owner sat. Uncle John always occupied the end seat of the family pew on the center church aisle, and after the minister had launched into his sermon, he settled himself comfortably and went to sleep, as did the mastiff, who lay under the pew.

One Sunday a lady parishioner, late for service, came tiptoeing hurriedly up the aisle followed by a tiny lapdog that paused to stick its nose under the pew to sniff at the mastiff who lay there asleep. It waked the mastiff, who sprang to his feet with a roar that shook the timbers of the church.

Uncle John also waked and he sprang up too, but instead of giving out a roar like the mastiff, he shouted, "Hell fire!"

The minister stopped preaching. The congregation turned to look at Uncle John, who, realizing what he had done, strove to get himself in hand.

Bowing to the minister with his usual dignity, he said, "Pray excuse me, Sir." Then, looking about at the startled congregation, he added, "Pray excuse me, one and all."

After this he settled himself in his accustomed place. The mastiff did the same; and no doubt, both of them went to sleep again.

As I grew older, I sensed that Aunt Claudia often felt lonely following the death of her husband, for they had been devoted to each other. I surmised that this accounted for the tea parties she often gave, especially on winter afternoons. To these she invited elderly ladies who had been her friends all during the long years, and she often suggested that I stop by after school if I wished to help Emma serve the refreshments—which I was delighted to do.

As the ladies sat snug and comfortable about Aunt Claudia's parlor fire and the wind raced across the lawn outside through the leafless trees, they reminisced and told stories of the past that I liked to hear. One of them was about a young Confederate soldier who had lived on a plantation in the valley not far from Morganton and had been killed at the battle of Gettysburg during the Civil War.

The story was that as he lay dying on the battlefield he found a twig lying nearby. He dipped it into "his heart's blood" and wrote on a piece of paper that he took from his pocket, "General, tell my father that I died with my face to the enemy."

All of the old ladies worshipped him as a hero, but one of them, who had obviously become a little less confused about past events than the teller of the story, said that the note was really written with a pencil, since in his dying condition it would have been impossible to write legibly with a wobbly twig. At once there arose some dissenting voices, she standing up for the pencil while a few other ladies held out for the twig. Some of them declared they felt certain they had seen the blood stained note written in his blood, and the writing was not at all wobbly. In fact, the young soldier's faithful body servant had brought it home to his father after the battle, along with his sword and gold watch. However, in the end the matter was settled amicably.

There was also a tale about another young gentleman who once lived in Morganton and whom all of the ladies seemed to adore. They said he was "tall, dark, and so charming and handsome that all the young ladies fell in love with him at first sight." He became a well-known journalist and writer and also "a brilliant career diplomat." He was sent to China as Assistant to the United States Consul, and there the Chinese ladies fell in love with him, too. One of them was the wife of a wealthy and powerful Mandarin, who became so jealous of the handsome young man that he vowed to have him murdered.

The Mandarin hired assassins to follow him about and on several occasions the young man barely escaped being caught and killed. Enraged by this, the Mandarin saw to it that the net was drawn so tightly about him that he had literally no chance of escape. The victim knew that his only hope of getting away was to leave China, so when he learned that a ship was sailing for the United States, he bought a coffin. He got into it and was smuggled aboard the ship. Thus, he escaped the Mandarin and arrived safely at home, where he continued to gain prestige in his profession and to attract the ladies—until he died in his late thirties.

He was buried in Morganton, where he was a member of a prominent family, and his funeral was attended by a large crowd from all over the state and elsewhere. Also in attendance were several young ladies who had dressed in mourning because they were deeply in love with him. They wore black dresses and widow's bonnets with long black veils that reached to their heels. When his coffin was being lowered into his grave, one of them, unable to restrain herself because of grief, rushed forward and had to be forcibly held back from casting herself upon the coffin, to be with him in death as she had hoped to be in life.

This created a most moving and spectacular drama that the little village was never to forget, and I thought it the most romantic and dramatic story that Aunt Claudia ever told me.

In the springtime there was a wide swath of bluebells under the trees across Aunt Claudia's front lawn. She always let me pick as many as I wished, and at times she invited me to tea parties for just the two of us. She had a whatnot in her parlor that was taller than I was at the time and it was filled with beautiful and valuable objects that I loved to look at and admired: miniatures of her ancestors painted on ivory; rare old silver and china snuffboxes; plates as delicate and thin as eggshells; and other bibelots.

Seated together like two ladies in her parlor—for she always treated me as though I were a grown up lady like herself—we drank tea that was thickly laced with cream and sweetened with lump sugar out of delicate and beautiful cups that had pastel flowers painted on the outside, and in the inside, too. Some of the cups had a pink rose painted in the bottom of the cup and I always drank until I finished the tea and made the rose appear.

She had a beautiful little rosewood spinet inlaid with satinwood in a bellflower design and she often played and sang for me after we had finished our tea party. When she sat playing, I thought she looked like a girl more than the old woman that she really was. The afternoon sunlight slanting through the tall windows gave her waving silver hair a glint of gold and her voice was a sweet, sometimes tremulous, soprano like that of a girl. We both liked the old Scottish songs: "Annie Laurie"; "The Bonnie Belle Brandon"; "Loch Lomond"; and "Flow Gently, Sweet Afton." She always added some songs of the Civil War, too: "Lorena"; "Somebody's Darling"; "The Blue and the Grey"; "Tenting Tonight"; and "Just Before the Battle, Mother." I liked to hear the latter two songs, but I thought they were very sad.

> *Just before the battle, Mother,*
> *I am thinking most of you.*
> *While upon the field we're marching*
> *With the enemy in view;*
> *Farewell, Mother you may never*
> *Press me to your heart again,*
> *For well I know that on the morrow*
> *I may be numbered with the slain.*

The saddest song of all, however, was "The Conquered Banner," the song of the Confederate flag, and sometimes I noticed that she shed a tear or two while she sang and played it. Its ending words were:

> *Furl that banner, softly, slowly;*
> *Treat it gently, it is holy,*
> *Touch it not, unfurl it never*
> *Let it droop there, furled forever*
> *For the people's hopes are dead.*

## Chapter Four

When she had finished singing, she would wipe away an extra tear and say, "We must think of something that is happier."

Then I would ask for a happier story and one of them that I liked was about the wedding reception of Governor Zebulon Baird Vance that took place at the old McDowell home in Quaker Meadows just across the river from town. I thought it a very romantic tale and it was also of special interest to me because Vance and his bride spent their bridal night after their wedding at my home one block up the street—the home in which I was born and in which I was living when Aunt Claudia told me the story.

"The reception was a delightful occasion," Aunt Claudia said. "But, just as it was ending, something happened that came close to turning it into a terrible tragedy, and it was a wonder that both the bride and groom escaped alive."

*The Wedding Reception of Governor Zebulon Baird Vance
— Lady La Poloma — The Fire Horses — The Angora
Goat — Two Different Trips To Town — Edward*

### 5.

The bride of Governor Zebulon Baird Vance was Miss Harriet Espy and their wedding reception was held at Quaker Meadows, the old historic home of the McDowell family in Quaker Meadows, just across the Catawba River from Morganton, on the afternoon of August 2, 1853.

Miss Espy, a relative of the McDowells, had been orphaned at an early age and had been taken into the McDowell home to live, so she was considered to be a member of the family. The wedding took place at twilight at the First Presbyterian Church in Morganton that in those days stood on West Sterling Street about a block from the Courthouse. It was a simple ceremony, with only the immediate members of the family present, but at the reception that was held just before the wedding at the McDowell home, there was a large number of guests.

After the bride and groom were ready to leave the reception and had gotten into a buggy to drive to Morganton for the wedding, the horse suddenly became frightened and dashed wildly down into the wide stretch of grassy meadowland in front of and below the house.

As the buggy careened swiftly down the hill at a terrific speed, the guests were certain that the vehicle would overturn and the couple would be killed—or drowned if the horse ran into the river. Just before the horse reached the water, however, Governor Vance, who was a man of powerful physique, was able to get control of the animal and he and his bride drove safely into Morganton to get married.

What interested me greatly about the story was that after they were married and left the church, they drove a few blocks further, turned into King Street, and spent their bridal night at Rose Villa, where I was born many years later and was still living when I heard this story. The town library now stands on that place but at the time of the Vance wedding it was the home of Mr. and Mrs. William McKesson, Mrs. McKesson being a cousin of the bride. I was intrigued by the fact that Vance and his bride spent the night there and I always wondered what room they occupied, but no one remembered.

## Chapter Five

It was about the time when I was growing older and no longer played some of my childhood games that I began to attend Aunt Claudia's tea parties, and it was also about this time that my father was searching for a suitable pony to buy for my younger brother. As he was driving by the Courthouse one day he saw that a crowd was gathered there and a number of horses and mules were on sale. The circus had come to town, had gotten into some sort of financial difficulty, and was selling the animals to pay its debts. It was then that my father saw Lady La Paloma. She was not a pony, but a beautiful little horse, not much bigger than a large pony, with a coat like black satin. He saw her good points at once and bought her on the spot.

Of course, we and all the children in the neighborhood fell in love with her on sight, and it was quickly obvious that she liked children as much as we liked her. We found her to be smart and obedient as well as beautiful, but it was not until some weeks later that we discovered that she possessed remarkable talents and attributes of which we were unaware. We discovered this one afternoon after school when I was laboriously practicing my piano lesson and my brother came running to tell me to hurry and look at Lady La Paloma because she was dancing about in the grazing lot.

By the time I reached her she had stopped dancing, but remembering that she was a circus horse gave me an idea. We hurried to put a record that played a rollicking tune on our Victrola and the little horse, on hearing the music, at once went into her act. Around and around the lot she went, prancing and dancing, rising on her rear legs, keeping step in time to the music while daintily pawing the air and bowing and tossing her head, as though she had ribbons and plumes upon it—which she had probably worn when she performed in the circus.

At the news of this, all the children in the neighborhood came running to watch her, along with grown people who were also fascinated by her antics. Then people from other parts of town began telephoning to ask the time of her next performance.

In response to all the interest that was shown, my father had Jim drive a short iron stake (to which an extra long rope could be tied that reached from the stake to her bridle) in the wide grassy space on our front lawn in front of the house. Then we played the Victrola and she went into her act. Passersby paused to watch and applaud and large groups of persons, young and old, came to observe her; and of course, we were proud of having such a talented horse.

There came a time, however, when we discovered that she was not as perfect as we had thought her to be at first. She had a way of lifting the latch on the gate between the grazing lot and the orchard, and when the weather grew warm, she'd lift the latch, dash down through the orchard, jump the back orchard fence and speed up the back alley to West Union Street a few blocks away.

In some way that we could not discern, she had found a place where West Union Street dipped down into a hollow of sorts that in dry weather was deep in thick yellow dust and after a rain became a large puddle of sticky red clay mud. There she joyfully flung herself down, rolling over and over and wallowing to her heart's desire, kicking her feet into the air, scattering dust or splashing mud. This stalled traffic and frightened passersby, and of course, our telephone began to ring as people called to report her carryings-on.

Naturally, all of this irritated Jim exceedingly. He would dash out to the stable, grab her bridle off its peg and set off at a run up the back alley to catch her, and we children would jog happily behind him, our dogs at our heels—just as we did when he ran up the alley with the wheelbarrow to ride Emma home when Aunt Claudia said she was "indisposed."

Lady La Paloma always allowed him to put on her bridle and she returned home as meekly as a lamb, but her shining black satin coat was covered with a thick layer of dust or roughened and matted with mud, so that she bore no resemblance to the beautiful little horse that had run away only a short time before.

Of course, she had to be given a bath at once—which irritated Jim still further—but all the neighborhood children pitched in to help with enthusiasm, scrubbing her off with soap and water and then spraying her with the garden hose—knowing that when we finished she would be beautiful again.

Unfortunately, it was the other way around with the town Fire Horses, a pair of once handsome dappled greys. They had grown so fat standing in their stable near the Courthouse, waiting for fires to break out, that we feared they could not reduce enough to look handsome again—and what was more important, to get to any fire on time. To give them much needed exercise, it was decided to put them to hauling loads to and from the train station.

Consequently, they were engaged in this work when the worst fire the village had ever known broke out. As quickly as possible, a man on horseback set off to find them. When they were found they were unhitched from the load they were hauling, galloped back to the fire station, hitched to the Fire Wagon and rushed to the fire—but by that time the house they had come to save had burned to the ground.

After this calamity the mayor asked for volunteer firemen. A number of young men responded to his call for help, and to my delight, our street was chosen as the best place for the fire drills. The volunteers drilled with a contraption called a fire reel that looked like a large spool with a wheel at each end and it had a long water hose wrapped about it.

Before a drill, which was really a race between the two teams into which the volunteers were divided, a line was drawn across the dusty street in front of the Episcopal Church just up the hill. Another line was drawn in front of the Baptist Church two blocks away toward the center of town.

A team stationed itself along the line in front of the Episcopal Church, and, at a signal, dashed down to the Baptist Church, pulling the fire reel behind it as it ran. The winning team was the one that could run more quickly to the Baptist hydrant, unscrew the cap on the hydrant, unwind the hose from the fire reel, screw its nozzle onto the hydrant, and send a stream of water jetting into the air. These races were well attended by ladies as well as gentlemen, since there was little other entertainment in town in the late summer afternoons when the drills took place. Each spectator had a favorite team and clapped and cheered as it sped along, followed by a cloud of dust and accompanied on the sidewalks on each side by small boys who raced excitedly along with an assortment of barking dogs.

The team that always won was captained by the handsome butcher (once the beloved of Polly Malindy) because he was a young man of such quickness and strength that he could unscrew the cap of the Baptist hydrant, clap the water hose onto it and hold it in place without screwing it on (which was against the rules) before sending a stream of water into the air. Not long after this, the fire drills that had offered welcomed entertainment to the village were stopped and we settled back into our usual quiet and uneventful routine—until my father sprang a surprise upon us for which we were altogether unprepared.

This was the purchase of a large pedigreed Angora ram that he bought to add to the flock of goats on a farm he owned about fifteen miles from town, a place we children liked to visit and which we called the Billy Goat Farm. The goat came by train in a box car and when he arrived at the depot, my father left his office and took us to see him in his gasoline machine, and what we saw was impressive as well as a little frightening, to say the least.

Standing at about the height of a Shetland pony, the animal had long, silky white fleece that reached to his ankles, a white beard, wickedly gleaming eyes, and ferociously curved horns. While he was waiting for the wagon to transport him to the Billy Goat Farm, he was kept tied on the platform at the depot, where a crowd gathered to look at him, since he was by no means a familiar sight.

After we took a long look at him and left, he managed to break the heavy rope with which he was tied, bounded off the platform, dashed through the railroad cut, and headed up the railroad tracks toward Asheville.

On being informed of this, my father quickly offered a substantial reward for his return and a crowd of men and boys began to search for him. One day went by with no sign of the goat. A second and a third day followed without any sign of him; so we decided the animal was destined to spend the rest of his life roaming the woods, mountains and valleys of the area—until on the fourth morning, when a startling event occurred.

Directly after breakfast on that morning Jim went to the stable to let Bucephalus out of his stall and into the grazing lot. Then he came running excitedly to tell my father that he had noticed the double front doors of the carriage house (where my father kept his automobile before a garage was built close to the house) were standing ajar. At this, he had peered inside and, to his amazement, saw the ram standing in its shadowy interior beside my father's gasoline machine.

On being told of this unexpected good fortune, my father quickly formulated a plan. He told Jim he would quietly enter the carriage house by its double front doors and close them behind him, shutting himself inside the carriage house with the ram. At the same time Jim would open the back double doors that gave onto the grazing lot, and quickly get out of the way—after which my father would attempt to drive the animal into the lot.

On overhearing this conversation, I thought this appeared to be a good plan, but in case there should be some unexpected and interesting development, I hurried to a spot outside the six foot high fence of planks that enclosed the lot and that ran all the way from the carriage house to one of the two back doors of our house. I found a knothole in the fence and there I stationed myself to observe whatever event might occur.

Through the knothole I saw Jim cautiously open the back doors of the carriage house and then leap to safety atop the fence—and not a moment too quickly, for the ram shot out into the lot as though propelled from a cannon. For a moment he paused, seeming to be bewildered by his sudden change of scene. Then he saw Bucephalus grazing peacefully nearby, unaware that danger lurked near, and at this, with blazing eyes and lowered head, he charged.

The big bay, suddenly alerted to danger, reared, wheeled and took off at a gallop, encircling the lot with the ram in full pursuit. Around and around they sped for several minutes until, as though at a signal, the horse wheeled again, planted his feet and faced the ram.

Then the race was reversed with the horse chasing the ram. The chase continued for a few minutes, when suddenly the ram, as though realizing he could not escape by jumping the six foot high plank fence that enclosed the lot, swerved in his flight and made for the only exit in sight, which happened to be the back door on that side of our house. It stood open and into it he shot, through the back hall and into the kitchen.

Before the entrance of the ram, the scene in the kitchen was one of tranquility. Alice, our cook, and Janie, my little brother's nurse (who had him with her at the time), had been told nothing about the ram and they were engaged in a desultory conversation while enjoying a second cup of breakfast coffee, but at the entrance of the ram, pandemonium broke out. From where I stood at the knothole in the fence, I could hear their wild whoops and yells as they grabbed up my brother and scuttled for safety, scrambling upstairs, where they shut themselves in a bedroom and fell upon their knees with loud lamentations and prayers.

Hearing the commotion they made, my mother, who had been told nothing about the ram, came at a run from another part of the house to find them, certain that some terrible catastrophe had occurred. On locating them and facing a locked door, she ordered them to stop the racket they were making, to unlock the door and to come forth; but this they refused to do. Nor would they rise from their knees as they continued in lamentations and prayer.

When my mother insisted on an explanation of their conduct, they informed her through the locked door that the devil had just visited them in the kitchen for the express purpose of carrying them off that very morning to the place to which, they were, naturally, least desirous to go.

She told them that the devil could not possibly have come into the kitchen, but they replied just as positively that it could be no one else—that they had recognized him the moment he appeared, that he was "unholy" to look upon, had horns and fiery eyes, and their hearts had failed them at the sight. When she finally persuaded them to unlock the door and come out of the room they were so weak that they could scarcely perambulate, and so fearful of the devil's return that they wept and mumbled in prayer as they wobbled down the stairs.

As for the ram, the bedlam in the kitchen had so bewildered him that he had wheeled and shot back into the lot, where he found the embattled Bucephalus awaiting him, and the chase had begun again. After it continued for a while, becoming even swifter and more astonishing, it took some expert maneuvering on the part of my father and Jim to get the situation in hand, but Bucephalus was finally put back into his stall and the ram was given the run of the lot until the wagon came to carry him off to the Billy Goat Farm.

When quiet was restored at last, we tried to solve the puzzle of how the ram happened to be on our premises when he could have had the pick of any other place in the whole area. We felt sure that the person who had put the animal in the carriage house was enjoying our puzzlement and would appear at any time to claim the reward my father had offered for the ram's return, but no one ever came, and to this day the mystery has never been solved.

As I grew still older, I did not lose my pleasure in going to visit my aunts in the country and I found it interesting while visiting them to come on errands to town with them from time to time. Usually the two ladies made the town trips together in the Low Buggy, with Aunt Matilda driving, but there were times when one sister went and the other remained at home. On these occasions I went along, and I found that the trips I made with Aunt Matilda were altogether different from those I made with Aunt Mary Lou.

Sometimes when Aunt Matilda and I went to town together and Aunt Mary Lou stayed at home, Aunt Matilda took advantage of the situation to impress upon me the importance of good manners, which, she said, she had found were sadly lacking in the young people of my generation.

She stated that our family, like other Southern families, had "fallen on hard times" after the war but that did not mean that we should

## Chapter Five

allow the "standard of good manners to go down." My mother sometimes lectured on this subject, too, but Aunt Matilda appeared to be even more strict in the rules she thought I should follow, which were those by which she and Aunt Mary Lou had been reared at a still earlier time.

She also said, "Water seeks its own level," and that "Birds of a feather flock together." She stated that, "The bottom rail was getting on top mighty fast," but that, "Blood still told." Nor was it only Aunt Matilda who held to such notions. I discovered that Aunt Creola and Uncle Ike expressed similar ideas when I chanced to hear them talking together, and in fact, they appeared to be even more caste conscious than Aunt Matilda.

"Better not any of these free issue folks come round me makin' a brag about befo' the war!" Aunt Creola said. "Ain't none of them cut high rye befo' the war in the olden days. I was right here then, just as I is now, and I knows who was who and what was what."

"I hears you talkin', Sis Creola." Uncle Ike would shake his head sadly about prevailing conditions and what the world was coming to. "The bottom rail's gettin' on top mighty fast and them what puts theyselves forward nowadays—why, none of them was quality and top drawer befo' the war."

"Quality!" Aunt Creola's lip would curl with even greater scorn. "You—Isaac—don't even let me hear you speak the word! Why, some of them was lower than a snake's belly in them olden times."

Aunt Matilda, like Aunt Creola and Uncle Ike, had been here before the war, too, and knew who was who and what was what. Although she agreed with Aunt Mary Lou that serving the Lord and going to heaven were the most important things of all, she stressed the fact that it was necessary while still on earth to have good manners and to conduct oneself as a lady and as a gentleman should.

She said that, when seated, a lady should never allow her back to touch the back of her chair—a rule that I thought was impossible to follow until I remembered that when she and Aunt Mary Lou were young ladies, they wore corsets stiffened with whale bone stays that enabled them to maintain such a position. She also said that the approved posture for a lady when walking in public was with head and shoulders erect and arms bent at the elbows, never hanging down at her sides. She added that when she and Aunt Mary Lou were girls, they had to walk back and forth across the floor with a book balanced on their heads to achieve this proper style of locomotion.

She impressed upon me, too, that a lady should never cross her legs at the knee but should sit with both feet upon the floor. She admitted there could be times when a lady grew tired of sitting in this position, so then she would be permitted to cross her legs at the ankle, although it was always "more seemly" to keep both feet upon the floor. In fact, she said, a lady should not even mention her legs, but, if she absolutely could not get out of doing so, she should refer to them as "limbs."

As we rode along comfortably in the Low Buggy as it swayed upon its coiled springs and little puffs of dust spurted up from its rubber-tired wheels, I could not help feeling proud of the old lady and the handsome buggy, too. The buggy was always kept in immaculate condition. The horse was carefully curried and the silver mountings on his bridle and harness had been polished so well by Uncle Ike that they glinted in the sun.

As for the old lady herself, she was always looking her best—even in her duster of tan-colored linen that she put on to shield her clothing from the dust of the road. I was also fascinated by the sheer tan-colored dust veil she tied over her bonnet that was like a large bubble and looked as though it could be whisked off at any moment by a sudden gust of wind. And, best of all, she smelled delightfully of violet cologne.

In town she greeted acquaintances she met in a cordial way, attended to her errands at the bank and the stores, briefly visited old friends and relatives (from whom she pleasantly and skillfully extracted all the news in town) and, just as she had left home at the time she had set for our departure, she returned promptly at the time she had set for our return.

Unfortunately, this could not be said of Aunt Mary Lou. When she and I went to town together, we did not follow the "new road" (that was so-called because it had been built since the Civil War), and we did not cross the river by the bridge that had been built upstream. Instead, for private reasons of our own, we chose the High Buggy in which to ride and we followed the "old road" that the family had used during and ever since the Revolutionary War, and we crossed the river at the wide old fording place.

When Aunt Mary Lou and I went to town she did not dress up as much as Aunt Matilda did. She wore her duster but she never tied a bubble-like veil over her hat. Instead she just mounted to the seat of the High Buggy, waited for me to scramble up beside her, and she even allowed me to go barefoot, which I loved to do, but of which

# Chapter Five

Aunt Matilda disapproved.

"It is certain to widen the feet," Aunt Matilda often said, "and what lady wants to go paddling through life on wide flat feet like a duck?"

Just before Aunt Mary Lou and I were ready to start for town, Aunt Matilda would say, "Now don't dawdle along the way, Mary Lou. Keep the horse at a good pace. Get the news. Tend to your errands and be sure to come home in time for dinner."

"All right, Matilda," Aunt Mary Lou would reply, clucking to the horse to get him started.

The old road that we travelled had fallen somewhat into disrepair because it was not used often after the new road was built, so the horse had to make his way carefully while the wheels of the High Buggy slipped into and out of ruts that made the buggy creak and groan as though it might come apart any moment. However, there were compensations along the way that Aunt Mary Lou and I pointed out to each other and enjoyed.

In the adjacent meadows there were misty white patches of Queen Anne's lace and whole areas of daisies that shimmered to dazzling whiteness in the sun. At the edges of the road small iridescent lizards sunned themselves and often a rabbit skipped along in front of us before scrambling into a thicket nearby. In the ditches on either side were trumpet vines with coral and flame-colored flowers, where hummingbirds hovered and darted; delicate tangles of golden Love Vines and May Pop blossoms, lavender and white.

After we had gone a mile, we came to the canebrake along the river and, as we drove down the sandy road that ran through it to the water's edge, we could hear the strange whispering sounds made by the paper-thin leaves of the cane as the river breeze crept through it.

If it happened to be the first crossing following the spring freshets, we knew it was best to proceed with caution for, as the black people on the place said, "The river was a sometime thing." During a spring freshet, it often changed its course here and there, which made a crossing more exciting but more dangerous, too.

The horse, sharing our apprehension, always stopped at the water's edge, shaking his bridle and looking up and down the river, as though communing with it, seeking to assess its changes and learn its new depths and shallows; and while he was doing this, Aunt Mary Lou let him take his time, waiting until he began his slow, cautious descent into the swift, ice cold water.

The deepest water was close to the bank where we entered it, but soon the riverbed began to slope upward to the wide sandy bar in the middle. The sandbar was covered by only about a foot of water and when the horse reached it, dragging the dripping buggy to stand upon it, he always stopped, for it was there that Aunt Mary Lou let me get out to wade.

While I waded about, sending minnows skimming about my feet, Aunt Mary Lou sat quietly in the buggy, enjoying the scene about her: the endless quivering of the green lace curtains that the willows along the banks let fall into the ever moving water; the quick silver leaping of a fish or the darting of a dragonfly, its wings iridescent in the patterned light. After I finished wading and climbed back into the buggy we often sat so quietly, just enjoying the scene about us, that herons flew down and walked about on the small, willow shrouded island just up the river or stood motionless on one incredibly thin leg, as though lost in thought.

Once Aunt Mary Lou told me that she never crossed through that river fording place that she did not think of Tennyson's beautiful poem, "The Lady of Shalott," that she had been made to memorize at boarding school. She told me the story of the poem and recited portions for me, her soft, old voice seeming to be a part of the murmuring voice of the river.

> *Willows whiten, aspens quiver,*
> *Little breezes, dusk and shiver*
> *Thro' the wave that runs forever*
> *By the island in the river*
> *Flowing down to Camelot.*

On one occasion after Aunt Mary Lou, at my request, had recited the poem, we suddenly realized that we must have lost quite a lot of time sitting there in the midst of the river and that Aunt Matilda had told us to return in time for midday dinner, and remembering this, Aunt Mary Lou hastily started the horse. Between the sandbar and the opposite bank we had to descend into deeper water again, and I am convinced that a child who has never forded a wide river with a sandbar in the middle in a high buggy has missed one of the most enjoyable and exciting experiences that childhood can offer. Merry-go-rounds, ferris wheels and roller coasters cannot offer half so many thrills.

When we returned much later to Bellevue, the moment we came

within sight of the house on the hill, we could see the plump figure of Aunt Matilda stationed on the front porch, impatiently awaiting us. She had her megaphone in her hand and the moment she glimpsed us she put it to use.

"Mary Lou!" she shouted, her voice reverberating across the bottom lands. "You're late for dinner!"

Spurred into action, Aunt Mary Lou made the horse go faster, but it was not fast enough to suit Aunt Matilda.

"Touch up the horse, Mary Lou!" she yelled. "Touch up the horse, Mary Lou-u-u!"

After we reached the house, Aunt Matilda scolded Aunt Mary Lou for being so late and I was thankful that she had not been able to see us sitting in the middle of the river while Aunt Mary Lou quoted "The Lady of Shalott" and I sat listening, spellbound by the beauty of the words and absorbed in the story. On that occasion Aunt Matilda was so annoyed at being delayed in getting her afternoon beauty sleep, she even forgot to ask about the news in town. In fact, it was not until the three of us were getting ready for bed that she remembered to do so.

"Well—yes," Aunt Mary Lou said when questioned about this. "I did hear something of interest. Augusta is in town, and Edward—he is too. It seems that Augusta is not well—so, on the doctor's advice, they plan to stay for the rest of the summer. He thinks she may benefit from the climate."

"Augusta's ill?" Aunt Matilda paused to ponder this bit of information. "But she's always been as strong as a horse. What seems to be the matter?"

"It's her heart, Mary Lettie says."

"Probably just a touch of dyspepsia," Aunt Matilda said. "I have it myself from time to time."

"But Mary Lettie says it might carry her off at any day."

Aunt Matilda put on her nightcap and tied the ribbons under her chin. "Did she happen to say how he is looking?"

"As handsome as ever," Aunt Mary Lou told her. "But, of course, time takes its toll."

"He's—bald?"

"Oh, no. Nothing like that. You remember what a fine suit of hair he had—a lovely light brown, and wavy, too. Mary Lettie says it's white now—a beautiful silver white."

Aunt Matilda considered this statement for a moment. "It makes him look very distinguished, I suppose."

"Mary Lettie says it does."

Already the night breeze was beginning to creep up the hill from the river and the curtains stirred in the misty-gold lamplight that filled the room. Aunt Mary Lou, as usual, looked out the window at the night, waited a moment and sighed.

"I know you don't like to speak about it, Matilda, but I somehow have the feeling that if anything should ever happen to Augusta—"

Aunt Matilda cut her off at once. "Now don't start on that, Mary Lou. Edward would never take it into his head to come to see me again."

But Aunt Mary Lou was right, I thought. There was something that suddenly let me know. Was it the look on Aunt Matilda's face—or the look on Aunt Mary Lou's? Beyond all doubting, I knew that the romance between Aunt Matilda and Mr. Ed Alston—that she had so hastily cut off so along ago—was going to bud and blossom again. Somehow—in some way—it was going to happen.

And time was to prove that I was right.

## Chapter Six

*Family House Parties — The Rites of Venus — "The Prime Totin' Man" — The Cave — "Going Adventuring" — Sarah's House — The Story Telling Hill — Flying Squirrels*

### 6.

Sometimes the invitations to visit my aunts in the country were prompted by the fact that they had decided to have a family house party, as they often did—which meant that relatives from other places would be on hand.

It was an unspoken rule that the children in the family should "get to know the kindred" and I found myself in full agreement with this idea; for the house parties under Aunt Matilda's skillful management not only afforded gastronomical delights, but also I enjoyed seeing the aunts, uncles and cousins who gathered on these occasions.

Due to business reasons, the three uncles, who were impressive looking gentlemen, all of them over six feet in height and well turned out with gold watch chains draped across their middles, could not come as often as the four aunts; but the aunts arrived regularly, bringing with them a number of offspring of different ages, sexes and sizes.

They came by train and in their arrival and departure Uncle Ike, who was proud of having been their father's carriage driver before and during the Civil War, played an important role. Uncle Ike and his wife Aunt Betsy had elected to stay on at Bellevue after the War, as had a number of other black people. We children were especially fond of the kind old couple.

We were impressed by Uncle Ike's expertise in matters of transportation; for it was he who saw to the "hitching up" and then drove the surrey to town to meet the train. On these occasions he dressed in his best, a black broadcloth suit of old-fashioned design, and placed upon his head a well brushed old-fashioned black silk top hat. Thus arrayed, he went to the carriage house and watched with a stern and exacting eye "the hitching up," which was done under his supervision by his grandson Tom, an indolent youth whom he was always urging to "step lively there!"

Sometimes the surrey could not hold all of the guests who were scheduled to arrive, so the carryall had to be sent to the depot, too, and there were several occasions when the Ship of Zion had to be put to use as well.

How this vehicle got its name I never knew. It was large and long and almost as old-fashioned as the closed carriage that was used before and during the Civil War and it still stood in the carriage house at Bellevue, gathering dust. It was a three-seater with a fringed canopy on top and the style-conscious Aunt Matilda was ashamed for it to even be seen upon the road. However, bowing to necessity, she had it cleaned up, given a coat of polish, and it went creaking into town behind the surrey and the carryall.

Because of the dusty unpaved roads, the vehicles had to be taken to town early, driven slowly and kept at a close and set distance from each other. This arrangement had to be followed to protect the passengers in the rear vehicles from the dust that was raised by the horses' hooves and the wheels of the vehicles in front. These trips to town took what seemed to be an interminable length of time, but finally the procession of vehicles would come into view in the distance, overflowing with relatives and followed by a cloud of dust. It would dip out of sight behind an intervening hill, reappear, and follow the long curve of the road through the bottom land before starting up the avenue.

Then what an exchange of greetings took place when it reached the house! Everyone was hugged and kissed and exclaimed over, often several times, and the children were sorted out and admired and told how much they had grown.

During these visits, Aunt Matilda, who was proud of her reputation as an excellent hostess and housekeeper, fairly "outdid herself." The meals were delicious and bountiful, always on time, and dinner and supper ended with old-fashioned desserts such as Tipsy Pudding, Charlotte Russe, Floating Island, Sillabub and Chocolate Blanc Mange with a large dollop of whipped cream on top.

At meals, everyone lingered long to enjoy the good food and to talk, and at night they gathered in the big lamplit parlor or on the shadowy front porch for still more talk, during which they reminisced. After I had gone to bed upstairs their voices and laughter floated up to me and I found it pleasant to lie in the darkness and listen, knowing that I was a part of the family, a member of the clan—a small and insignificant member, it was true, but nonetheless, a part of the whole and therefore possessed of a certain value in my own small way.

In remembering this now, I cannot help wondering if this pleasant sense of security and belonging may be lacking in many of the

## Chapter Six

children of today whose families are smaller and scattered, and whose family ties may not be strong.

During these visits, there must have been at least a few annoyances and a small misunderstanding or two, but if so, I was never aware of it. What I remember was the pleasure they took in the company of each other—and also the talking, the laughter, and the reminiscing that never ceased.

Although I enjoyed the family gatherings, the visits that afforded me even more pleasure were those when I was the only guest; for it was then that each lady felt free to follow her usual daily routine, and this gave me the opportunity to know them more intimately and to take their true measure.

When I was the only houseguest, directly after breakfast Aunt Matilda, who was proud of her looks, went into the downstairs bedroom that she shared with Aunt Mary Lou. She put on a pink silk "boudoir cap" trimmed with ribbons and lace to protect her hair and a large white apron that had been made to protect her dress. She washed her face in the big china bowl on the washstand in the corner, although she had already washed it before going in to breakfast. (Indeed, what lady did not?) Then, determined that her fine and girlish complexion would continue to be admired by all who looked upon it, she began her daily morning beauty ritual.

In this, her adoring black maid, Estelle, served as a dedicated acolyte. (Aunt Mary Lou did not have a personal maid because she was free of rheumatism and liked to do things herself.) When it was time for Aunt Matilda's beauty ritual to begin, Estelle placed in front of her mistress a small round-topped table that was reserved for that purpose and the rites that followed varied from day to day, depending upon what lotions, salves and ointments Aunt Matilda thought were needed for her complexion at that particular time.

Few cosmetics could be bought in that day (ladies sometimes even pinched their cheeks to make them pink), so Aunt Matilda's had to be mostly homemade. Sometimes she applied to her face a masque of cucumbers chopped in lemon juice and sometimes a mixture of egg whites whipped to a froth with crushed almonds added. Sometimes she chose a paste of buttermilk or cream or cornstarch or oatmeal and other ingredients, but for the beautification of the hands, she used glycerine and rose water. She said she'd rather have a pretty hand than a pretty face, but I noticed that she labored earnestly to preserve and embellish both.

The whole ceremony was intriguing to watch, but if I lingered near I was told to soak my fingers in the glycerine and rose water and then to pinch the ends to make them taper as Aunt Matilda did. Nor did it end with this. She plastered the masque du jour over the freckles on my nose and warned me never to go out into the sun without a parasol or hat or sunbonnet, lest I ruin my complexion beyond repair. Consequently, I stayed out of her reach when the daily beauty ritual was in progress.

While Aunt Matilda was thus engaged in the bedroom, Aunt Mary Lou was equally busy but in a different way; for that was the time she had set aside to read her Bible and Prayer Book and to say her morning prayers. Our family prayed every day—before meals and at bedtime—but Aunt Mary Lou appeared to think we needed more praying over than that. Perhaps she knew of discrepancies in the behavior of certain relatives that Aunt Matilda was able to gloss over or did not know about. At any rate, after breakfast, she went into the parlor, closed the door and took the matter in hand.

Sometimes I wondered if she ever called the attention of the Lord to the rites of Venus then going forward in the bedroom, which possibly might be construed to mean that Aunt Matilda had not altogether forsaken the world, the flesh and the devil. However, being the kind and forgiving soul that she was, she may have felt that the good looks of Aunt Matilda, being God given, deserved such care and attention. Regardless of the reason, Aunt Mary Lou did have a long list of persons for whom to pray, since our family, which was large to begin with, seemed to be growing steadily, due to marriages and births.

Once when Aunt Mary Lou stayed in the parlor praying longer than usual, Aunt Matilda said she wondered if she called the family role and prayed for each member in turn, checking them off on the list as she went, with extra time allotted to the most hardened sinners, of course. However she managed it, Aunt Mary Lou's prayers did seem to take up a lot of time to me—a small restless girl who at that time every morning had to entertain herself without the help of either aunt while the beauty rites and praying were in progress.

Seeking diversion, I went to the poultry lot to visit the chickens, turkeys and guineas. The guineas I found particularly interesting as they scurried about calling out "par-track-par-track" and looking like little old ladies hunched over under black, white spotted shawls. Sometimes I went to see the horses and mules that were not in service at the time or to watch the cows, calves, sheep and lambs.

There were times, too, when I followed the peacocks that strutted proudly about the front lawn. These proud and beautiful birds were a delight to watch and I found it remarkable that they made better watchmen than any dog upon the place. They slept at night in the trees about the house and when a stranger, human or animal, came upon the premises they uttered their loud and raucous cries that sounded more like those of a tiger or some wild jungle beast than of a petted domestic fowl.

By the time I returned to the house, Aunt Matilda had finished her beauty routine and set the servants to their different tasks, and the household machinery was running smoothly under her capable management. Vegetables had been brought from the garden with the dew still glistening upon them and a boy had probably been sent to the cultivated berry patches for berries or to the grape arbors for grapes. A man might also have been dispatched to the mill on the place for fresh corn meal to make the muffins and spoon bread that Aunt Matilda enjoyed, and she herself may have gone into her flower garden to cut flowers, wearing a broad rimmed hat and gloves.

She enjoyed cutting out tea cakes and gingerbread men for the children, who often came calling with their elders. The cook made the dough for these and rolled it out on a big white marble slab that was kept in the kitchen for that purpose. Then Aunt Matilda went to work. For the tea cakes she pressed a large biscuit cutter into the dough, but for cutting out the gingerbread men, women, boys and girls—and she often cut out birds and animals, too—she used a small, sharp knife. Thus, each creation, having been fashioned as her whim directed, was different from its fellows and seemed to possess a personality of its own.

The cook made the batter for the layered cakes that were always kept on hand and Aunt Matilda enjoyed spreading icing on them. She never failed to leave some icing in the bowl for the two of us to share, and this we did, dipping in with tablespoons; for icing eaten in this manner somehow tasted even better than it did when on a cake.

Since early morning the tenants on the place, both white and black, had been at work in the low lying bottom lands, and if Aunt Matilda wished to question one or give an order, she went to the front or back porch, carrying her big metal megaphone. Her voice carried well through the instrument and she would call out the tenant's name, requesting him to come to the house. At this, one of the figures working in the wheat or corn rows in the bottom lands below would leave a horse and plow in a field or put aside his hoe and start up the hill to the house—after which it became evident from the conversation that followed that Aunt Matilda had a "head for business," knew the prices of wheat, corn, potatoes, and other crops, and also took a lively interest in all that was going on upon the place.

In fact, as an admiring tenant once said, "Miss Matilda always knew what she was talking about."

Sometimes, for the sheer pleasure of being a part of a delightful summer morning, she would sit rocking on the front porch for a short interval, and at such times a black tenant's wife might come up the hill, bringing a baby.

"Miss Matilda, I'se fit to be tied with this here chile. She been hollerin' so much I believes she's got the liver growing."

"Well, what have you done for her?" Aunt Matilda might ask in her brisk, capable way.

"I'se done what I'se always did. I'se took her by the feets and I'se swung her north and I'se swung her south. I'se swung her east and I'se swung her west. But it ain't done her no good."

"Well, maybe she has a sore throat," Aunt Matilda would suggest. "I'll take a look."

Later, after more questions and answers, the mother and child would depart with a bottle of medicine or a jar of salve from Aunt Matilda's medicine cabinet or with instructions to go to the doctor in town, with whom Aunt Matilda had made an appointment by telephone.

Sometimes it was the wife of a white tenant who came up the hill with a problem she wanted to discuss or some news she wanted to impart, and often she brought, as a gift, a small bunch of flowers from her garden.

"Miss Matilda, I've brung you a flower pot."

"Why that's certainly nice of you," Aunt Matilda would say. "How is your family getting along?"

"Tolerable well, thank the Lord—and I thought as how you might like to know that my youngest daughter has started to walkin' out."

With the tenant folk, especially those from the mountains, "walking out" and courting were the same, so at the mention of romance, Aunt Matilda perked up, as usual.

"You don't say! I didn't know she had caught a beau."

"Yessum. She's took up with a town fellow. He's sparkin' her regular and he looks ripe for the pickin'."

"Then you'll be having a wedding soon. How nice!"

"Yessum. And I'm only hopin' he'll turn out to be as good a toter as my older daughter's husband. Every time she looks out the door, he's comin' home a-totin' somethin'. If it ain't sugar, it's coffee. If it ain't coffee, it's salt or tea or somethin' else what's needful."

"I'm glad to know your older daughter's husband has turned out to be such a good provider," Aunt Matilda would say. "By the way, I have a pretty little embroidered handkerchief your younger daughter might like to carry when she goes walking out with her beau."

She would tinkle the little silver bell she kept beside her to summon Estelle to get the handkerchief, who always appeared promptly like a well rehearsed genie and carried out her bidding.

After Aunt Mary Lou had finished her prayers in the parlor, she would try to catch up on her reading, for she read constantly and liked to learn from the newspapers what was going on in the nation and the world. She also enjoyed rereading the classics. Hume's history of Scotland was one of her favorites, since it was from Scotland that many of her ancestors had come. She often read the works of Josephus, the Jewish historian who lived at the time of Jesus Christ and sometimes wrote about Him.

When the weather was good, she like to set up her easel upon the lawn and paint the mountains and the bottom lands, where the green of the meadows and the fields of corn and wheat accentuated the russets and browns of the ploughed lands in between. She particularly liked to paint Grandfather Mountain, which resembled so closely the profile of an old man lying on his back with his face upturned to the sky.

Around the noontime dinner hour the postman came on horseback from town twice a week, his saddlebags bulging with mail to be distributed about the countryside. At this, both ladies stopped whatever they were doing to enjoy the letters that came often from their sisters, for all of them liked to keep in touch and to know what was going on amongst the various members of the clan.

When the mail had been read and the noontime meal was over, Aunt Matilda would go into her bedroom, take off her corset, put on a silk wrapper and climb aboard the big soft featherbed to take her afternoon beauty nap. After this, the whole sun-filled afternoon belonged to Aunt Mary Lou and me, and it was then that we "went adventuring," which, as I grew older, became one of my greatest pleasures when I was visiting at Bellevue.

When we were ready to start, Aunt Mary Lou would say to me, "Go get your sunbonnet and I'll get the little round basket."

It was Aunt Matilda, ever mindful of the complexion, who had the pink gingham sunbonnet made for me, and the little round basket was for carrying all the treasures we anticipated finding that afternoon. Often we went first to the Gold Gully, the deep red clay ravine that split the woodland and tapered down into the bottom land near the creek. A few nuggets of gold had been found there in the past, but, although we searched diligently, all we ever found were some small glistening stones. Was it gold that made them glisten or only isinglass? I preferred to think it was gold, so we put them in the little round basket.

I never failed to be impressed by the agility with which Aunt Mary Lou climbed the steep sides of the Gold Gully, her long skirts swishing about her feet. When I commented upon this, she said she "was thankful that the Lord in His mercy had granted her to continue to be fleet of foot in her old age."

Going deeper into the woods, we sometimes sought out the grapevine swing that hung from a giant oak tree on the steep side of a wooded hill. It was really several large grapevines that had grown together, and at the bottom it curved out and then upward, making a perfect seat for a little girl to sit upon. Then, as I swung out above the rhododendron thicket that covered the hillside below, I could glimpse the creek glittering through the trees, and, if it happened to be early summer, I could see below me a cascade of rose and pink rhododendron blossoms in full bloom.

Down the hill near the creek there were whole areas of Trilliums that grew in the shade of the trees, and Aunt Mary Lou said that these three-leaved plants with their dainty white and purple lily-like blossoms stood for the Trinity: Father, Son, and Holy Spirit.

In a little dell close by we could find Lady Slippers, pink and yellow; wild Lilies of the Valley, Rosebud Orchids; and other wild flowers. Aunt Mary Lou, who knew the names of most of them, would gather some and put moss about the stems. She would go to the nearby creek and send minnows darting here and there in the clear, cold shallows while she scooped up water to moisten the moss. Then she would put them carefully into the little round basket, to be planted in the garden at home.

After this, we often climbed to the Rock House, the small cave in the steep hillside overlooking the creek, and on reaching it, we sat

## Chapter Six                                                                 145

down to rest on a large flat rock at the entrance that seemed to have been made for that purpose. In the damp earth inside the cave were prints of foxes' feet. The foxes never came up to the house anymore, but Aunt Mary Lou said that when she was young they could be seen often about the place—along with deer, and even bears—and sometimes they would slip into the poultry yard and steal a hen or two.

While we were resting on the big flat rock outside the cave, she told me tales about how "our men, the patriots" had hidden there with their horses to escape from the Tories during the War of the Revolution. Her ancestor had been with them, she said, and the house where he and his young wife, Sarah, lived so long ago—the home where Sarah met her death by trying to protect a wounded patriot—once stood just across the creek.

Talking of Sarah and that terrible event, we crossed the swinging bridge over the creek and visited the site of her home. The house had long since disappeared and the area had become a cornfield, but when the earth was freshly ploughed and no corn was standing, parts of the foundation were still visible, and we could see that it had been a large rectangular structure with a chimney at each end.

What had she been like, I wondered—that young wife named Sarah—who lived in that unforgotten house so long ago? Like a pale shadow, she seemed to walk beside us, stepping across the furrows, her baby in her arms. And where had the weave house stood—where she was struck down by the Tory's sword and lay bleeding from her fatal wound?

Young though I was, I sensed a sadness about the place and Aunt Mary Lou obviously sensed it too. It caused us to move more slowly and talk more quietly as we walked about. It held us in a spell, from which it did not release us until we had re-crossed the swinging bridge and reached the grassy bottom lands on the other side of the creek. According to tradition, those grassy meadows were once the scene of a bloody battle between the Catawba and Cherokee Indians, and the many Indian arrowheads that we found there and put in the little round basket seemed to confirm that this story was true.

There was a hill we liked to climb, especially in summer when it was covered with wild violets and pansies. We picked the flowers as we climbed until we had a bunch large enough to take to Aunt Matilda, who loved flowers of every sort. When we reached the top, we sat down to rest, lapped about by a lavender-blue tide of flowers, and it was from that hilltop that we could look down upon our favorite stretch of bottom land—a view that was at its best when the wheat fields below were greening or ripening into harvest.

When the wheat was greening and the river breeze swept over it, it rippled and tossed in long running waves like the sea, with troughs of deeper green in between; and when it was ripe it was a tossing golden sea. Sometimes we sat in silence, just watching it, but usually Aunt Mary Lou told me stories that the surrounding landscape brought to her mind. Because of this, I called that place the "story telling hill."

One story was about a close relative of ours who once lived across the river at his home that was called Belvedere. She said that after his wedding, when he and his bride started off on their wedding trip, the carriage suddenly stopped, so the groom called up to the coachman on the high box seat in front, asking what had happened.

"Look yonder, master." The coachman pointed to a mother quail, followed by sixteen little quails crossing the road in front of the carriage, "That's a sign you gwine have sixteen children." And this prophecy came true.

There was another story about the same kinsman when he was an old man on his deathbed. Aware that his death was imminent, his family had gathered about him, which was the custom of that day, when suddenly the old man roused and indicated that he had something to say.

His grandson, Waighstill Avery, went to his bedside and heard him say in a feeble voice, "King William is dead."

The family, thinking him delirious, paid little heed to this pronouncement—until some weeks later when word came by ship from England that the English king had died; and, in so far as it could be estimated, his death had occurred close to the time of the deathbed statement made by the dying man.

Another tale I liked to hear was about a young wife, Mrs. Grace Greenlee Bowman, who, while her husband was away from home fighting in the Revolutionary War, dreamed one night that he had been wounded on the battlefield. Although her family tried to stop her, she left home at once to go to him, carrying her small daughter in front of her on the saddle of her horse.

After riding about fifty miles through woods, rivers, and rugged terrain, she reached the battlefield and found her husband wounded, as in her dream. She did her best to help him, but in spite of this, he died. This was a sad story but one with a happy ending; for later on, she married Charles McDowell and came to live in his home in Quaker Meadows, which was about a mile from where we sat on the hill.

Aunt Mary Lou also told me that there was a road nearby that led over the mountains into Tennessee. It had begun as an old Indian trading path and there were Drovers' Places along the way because it was traveled by Drovers—men who drove animals on foot to market at Camden, South Carolina and even to the faraway Charleston market by the sea: horses, mules, cattle, sheep, and even turkeys.

She said that her father had taken her to see a nearby Drovers' Place just up the road when she was a little girl and there was lodging and food for the Drovers and also pens and provender for the animals and flocks of turkeys. The men usually stayed at these places long enough to keep the stock fat, so that they would sell well at market. She was interested in the fact that when they were ready to leave, the Drovers ran the turkeys through a wide vat of melted tar and then through a sand pit to coat their feet and keep them from wearing out before they reached market.

Sometimes when we were ready to leave the "story telling hill" and the scenery about us seemed to be particularly beautiful, Aunt Mary Lou would linger a few moments to appreciate it a little longer, and would repeat a quotation from the Bible. One of her favorites was, "The heavens declare the glory of God and the firmament showeth His handiwork." And sometimes she said, "Look about you child. This is the garden spot of the earth."

As we went up along the pasture fence, Clock, the big bay horse, often came to put his head over the top railing to be petted, his coat shining red-gold in the tinted light. High on the hill, the old home also seemed to be waiting for us, its windows aflame with the sunset. Aunt Matilda was waiting, too, and she was always puzzled as to why we had stayed away so long.

"Where on earth have you been all this time?" she would ask.

For this question we could never give what she considered to be a satisfactory reply. After all, who can put into a sentence or two all the sights, sounds, colors, emotions and pleasures of such a summer afternoon? Instead of trying to frame an answer, we gave her a large bouquet of wild violets and lavender-blue pansies that we had picked on the hill and let her and Estelle look at the treasures we had brought home in the little round basket.

After supper the ladies liked to sit on the shadowy front porch, where a nice breeze was blowing. It was then that the flying squirrels, that I never saw in town, came out from the trees on the lawn to play, and it was great fun for a child to watch these quaint little creatures who were so shy in the daytime but could put on quite a performance as dusk began to fall. Spreading their furry webbed legs that made them look as though they had wings, they flew from tree to tree in the twilight, somersaulting in midair and often darting to limbs where they cavorted and danced about in a ridiculous fashion. That was also the time when the lightening bugs came out. These we had in town, but not the myriads of magical ever-moving lights that glimmered across the lawn at Bellevue.

From where we sat looking down from the hilltop, the whole night seemed to be caught in a net of stars, for the skies were filled with them. The bottom lands far below were often covered by a sea of smoke-colored fog that glistened to silver here and there in the light of the moon while the mountains that surrounded the valley stood out starkly against the star flecked sky.

Aunt Matilda and Estelle were excellent singers and liked to sing together as they sat on the porch at night, and Aunt Mary Lou and I sang with them as well as we were able. Estelle was in the choir at Willow Tree Colored Baptist Church and she sang what she called "lead" and "short stop," while Aunt Matilda accompanied her in her resonant alto. Their songs were different from those of the soft voiced Aunt Claudia, for they liked to sing the vigorous rousing, old-fashioned hymns one seldom hears in church today: Onward Christian Soldiers"; "Shall We Gather at the River?"; "Roll, Jordan, Roll"; and "A Mighty Fortress is our God."

From the creek and river banks there lifted a cacophony of frog voices and Estelle said the reedy piping of the little frogs was asking, "How deep? How deep?" while the heavy basso of the bullfrogs was replying, "Knee deep, knee deep!" And if one listened carefully, that really did seem to be what they were saying.

From the woods there came to us from time to time sounds I never heard in town: the shrill, penetrating cry of a screech owl and the low, always eerie voice of a hooting owl. Sometimes the moon had a yellow haze encircling it that Estelle called a "rain ring." She said it was "a sure sign it was coming on to rain." She also said that if a wren "hallowed three times in a row, that was a sure rain sign, too."

If it rained we went to the parlor and played the gramophone. It was a big mahogany box with a large horn atop it that was shaped like a morning glory flower in full bloom. It played old-fashioned songs that the ladies liked: "The Turkey in the Straw"; "My Old Kentucky Home"; and "Way Down Upon the Swanee River." There were other records that played operas both sisters seemed to enjoy: "Carmen," "Rigolello," and "Die Meistersinger."

Some of the other melodies that we played on the gramophone made good music for dancing, and Aunt Mary Lou taught me the steps of some of the dances that were popular when she and Aunt Matilda were girls. We danced the Mazurka, the Lancers, the Schottische and did as well as we could with the Virginia Reel, although there were only the two of us.

"Heel and toe and one-two-three!" Aunt Mary Lou would call out as we dipped and glided across the parlor floor. "Heel and toe and away we go!" As I tried to keep in step with her I marveled at the graceful way her tall, slender figure swayed and turned as easily and gracefully as a girl's.

Aunt Matilda had once loved to dance and would have liked to join us, but her rheumatism would not permit her to do so. Consequently, she made up our audience along with the family portraits that looked down upon us from the parlor walls, and Estelle, who claimed she could do a "mean stomp at a chitlin' strut but wasn't much good at white folkses' dancin'."

At ten o'clock we began getting ready for bed as usual, but there was one night when the sisters took longer than usual to undress and their conversation was even harder for me to understand than when they talked about Mr. Ed Alston and the time when he "addressed" Aunt Matilda.

"It would just break my heart!" Aunt Matilda said.

Break her heart? I perked up at once and began to listen more closely.

"The Lord will not permit it," Aunt Mary Lou replied firmly.

"How can you say that so surely, when you know very well that—"

"Hush, Matilda. We'll say so more tonight. You must put it in the hands of the Lord and get a good sleep tonight. Then in the morning we'll have prayers again. Don't ever forget that the Lord moves in mysterious ways His wonders to perform."

"That I know, Mary Lou. Still—"

Aunt Mary Lou, noting my worried look and seeing that I was about to question her, turned to me.

"Don't worry, child. Everything, with God's help, will come out all right. We'll tell you all about it in the morning."

*A Heart-Breaking Scheme — Going to Willow Tree
Colored Baptist Church with Estelle — Edward —
A Shocking Plan*

### 7.

When I learned about the problem that had upset my aunts so greatly, I became upset, too. They told me that the local power company had decided to buy thousands of acres of valley land and to flood the valley, with the idea of generating more electricity. I knew from experience how flood waters looked and the damage they could do, and I imagined with horror the old brick home on the hill sinking slowly down into a relentless mud colored sea that surged about it and then covered it completely, so that it would always remain forever hidden under the water, never to be seen again.

"Will the water come up so high that it will really cover the house?" I asked, horrified at the thought.

The sisters, hastening to console me, told me that from all they could find out, the hill was too high to be covered. Instead, it would be like an island in a huge lake. They said that, because of the high prices for the land that the power company was offering to pay, there were a few persons who were willing to sell, but the owners of the old homes, descendants of early pioneers, were determined not to give in. Nor were Aunt Mary Lou and Aunt Matilda, as well as all of their brothers and sisters—who also loved the old home place dearly. If there were more persons who refused to sell than those who agreed to do so, the valley could be saved, they said.

"I'm sure we'll win!" said Aunt Matilda, who was becoming more optimistic about the situation. "We'll fight them, tooth and nail!"

"The prayers of a righteous man availeth much," added Aunt Mary Lou, quoting from the Bible, "and I'm sure the Lord will hear our desperate pleas."

As the ladies said, so it turned out. After many months of conferences, arguments and some litigation at the court, the catastrophe was averted. The power company resorted to other measures for generating electric power, and conditions became normal again.

Throughout the years that I visited at Bellevue, I was always allowed to go with Estelle to attend Sunday afternoon services at Willow Tree Colored Baptist Church just up the river when I wished to do so.

Sometimes instead of just "having preaching," the church held what were called "praise and shout services." These I especially enjoyed and, as I look back across the long years, I remember one that turned out to be different from any that preceded or came after it, and it took place on a beautiful Sunday afternoon in June.

That afternoon the sisters had gone to church in town in the Low Buggy with Aunt Matilda driving. They had stayed for Sunday Dinner at my house, and after returning home, Aunt Matilda had gone to her bedroom to take her afternoon beauty nap while Aunt Mary Lou took up a religious periodical to read.

As Estelle and I started down the back steps to go to Willow Tree Church we ran into Aunt Creola, the cook at Bellevue who had lost her box of "Delicious Lily Rose Snuff," and was returning to find it and also to help serve refreshments to the guests who were coming out from town that afternoon.

"Is you-all headin' for Willow Tree?" she asked with surprise.

"We're going to the Praise and Shout," I informed her.

"No, you ain't," she replied. "There done been a change in the program."

"What sort of change?" Estelle demanded.

"In case you ain't heard tell—Sis Beadie, what lives over at the Ransom place—she done upped and died and they gwine funeralize her this very afternoon."

Estelle stopped and pondered, "How you know?"

"Because I knows. I'm only surprised you ain't heard nothin' about it." Aunt Creola paused and added, "Well, go 'long if you will. I just hope you won't run into the devil while you be there."

She went into the house and I looked at Estelle. "Will the devil really be at Willow Tree?" I asked.

"Well, some folks say the devil done laid his hand on poor old Beadie," she confessed. "But she can't help bein' the way she turned out to be because it was the good Lord Hisself that made her that way. She just strange—not like other folkses—but she ain't never hurt nobody that I knows about."

"But suppose the devil's there?"

"Then this here's one nigger what's goin' to git outer there mighty fast." Estelle laughed at my frightened look. "Come on, honey. Don't pay no mind to what Sis Creola say. We done started, so let's go." As we went down to the barn lot, she added, "I think I'll drive Ole Pal. I've done driv him so much, it's like him and me has come to understand one another."

This appeared to be true by the way the big mule came at her bidding and backed between the shafts of the High Buggy, to which she hitched him. She helped me into the buggy and climbed in on the other side.

Ole Pal started down the narrow dusty road that led to the fording place in the creek, his broad rear quarters swaying majestically in front of us as we rode along. She let him stop for a drink when we reached the water. Then we crossed over to the opposite bank, where he suddenly stopped.

"What now?" Estelle flapped the buggy reins across his back and spoke as to the air.

She flapped the reins again over his back, but he remained standing as still as a graven image. Then I saw it—a large brown and grey "old field" rabbit, sitting upright upon its haunches on the right hand side of the road just ahead of us.

"The rabbit," I said.

"Say which?" Estelle glanced quickly about and caught sight of it. "That's a mean rabbit. He just sittin' there on purpose to put a spell on us. Ole Pal, he got sense." She stood up in the buggy and swung her arms in a threatening way. "Git!" she shouted at the rabbit. "Git back in the bushes where you come from, you limb of Satan!"

The rabbit kept an unblinking, steady eye upon us but did not move. Neither did Ole Pal, at which Estelle grumbled, "Now I got to git down and drive him off. Iffen I don't, he's liable to jump right across in front of us. Then there'll be trouble for shore."

At this, the rabbit sprang into the air and crossed the road ahead of us in two long jumps before disappearing into a thicket on the other side.

"You see how many jumps he took?" Estelle asked. "Two in all. That means we'll have two troubles before this day is done, and the first is we'll be late for the funeralizin'."

She was right. Already we could hear the distant strains of "Steal Away to Jesus" pouring out from the direction of Willow Tree Church, that stood on a low knoll near the river. It was made of wood that had never been painted, had weathered to a soft silver-grey, and stood in the embrace of a large clump of willow trees that clustered about it.

As Estelle urged Ole Pal onward, a woman's high sweet soprano voice keened through the door and windows that had been left open against the heat, soaring skyward like a bird.

## Chapter Seven

*My Lord calls me—*
*He calls me in the thunder—*
*The trumpet sounds in my soul.*

At this, the whole congregation joined in, male and female voices weaving together in a soul-moving tide of melody that flowed like a river down across the surrounding fields and meadows.

*The trumpet sounds in my soul—*
*Ain't got long to stay here—*

Estelle hastily tied Ole Pal to a willow sapling near the door and we found the church packed, as hot as an oven, and pasteboard fans (upon which was printed, "Glorious Rest Funeral Home, Corner of Green and Winter Streets") were waving rapidly everywhere, as though run by electric batteries. Estelle grabbed a fan from the rack inside the door and looked about, but there was not a seat in sight. Then her eye fell upon a tall young usher seated on the end of the bench just inside the door.

She gave him a quick poke with the fan and hissed, "Git up, boy—so me and the chile can set!"

Startled, he sprang to his feet and, pushing me ahead of her, she quickly slid into the small amount of sitting space he had left. She joined heartily in the singing, plying the fan so that its breeze caught both of us. I viewed the open coffin in front of the pulpit which was surrounded by flowers plucked from gardens, fields, and meadows, and was glad that from where we sat the deceased could not be seen.

The singing ended and then the shiny black bald head of the Reverend Bascomb suddenly loomed up in the pulpit.

"We are gathered here together to pay our respects and say farewell to our dear departed brother," he intoned in sepulchral tones suitable for the occasion—at which Estelle stopped fanning and I felt her stiffen at my side.

She placed the fan over our faces, so we could whisper in private. "What them last words you hear him say?"

"Our dear departed brother," I whispered back.

She thought this over briefly, then said, "Lean over and ask that fat lady on the other side of you who for this here funeral is."

I was squeezed so tightly between them that it was impossible to lean in any direction, but I looked up at the woman, who was fanning vigorously while rivulets of perspiration ran down her face, and caught her eye.

When I repeated Estelle's question, she placed her fan at the right angle for whispering and replied, "Honey, I don't know. I just got here myself."

I relayed her message to Estelle, who waited a moment and then whispered, "Well, listen close and see what do he say next."

Then the same words came again, "... our dear departed brother."

The young usher was standing in the aisle beside Estelle and she gave him such a sharp jab with her elbow that he jumped.

"Move over and git outer the way, so me and the chile can leave!" she ordered.

He jumped aside quickly. Estelle grabbed me and we hurried out into the bright summer afternoon.

"Well, Sis Beadie sholy ain't no dear departed brother," she announced as she lifted me into the buggy. "If Sis Creola is right and Sis Beadie is bein' funeralized today, it must be over at the Oak Ridge Methodist. Somebody ought to have told me her and the Reverend Bascomb had fell out agin. She all the time switchin' back and forth." She sighed and clambered into the buggy on the other side. "Well, Oak Ridge is more than twelve miles away. We'd never git there in time. So there ain't no use to try."

She headed Ole Pal back down the road along which we had just come, tied the reins around the buggy whip, which was in its holder on the dashboard, and let him go at will since he knew the way home and needed no guidance.

When we got back to the house on the hill we could hear Aunt Creola in the dining room where she was helping Aunt Matilda to put away cake plates and cut glass tumblers that were used in serving the guests who came out from town while we were away.

"Well, he's still a mighty fine lookin' gentman," I heard Aunt Creola say. "He's so rich lookin' about the head. How come he been out here to see you 'long with the ladies—but without his wife?"

"He and his wife are visiting in town," Aunt Matilda told her. "But she isn't well. She was taking a nap and he was sitting alone on the front porch—so the ladies stopped and asked if he'd like to ride out here for a little call."

"Well, it always seemed to me he was the best lookin' gentman caller you ever had, Miss Matilda, and you had a passel of 'em, too—but I nebber could see as how you could let Miss Gusta grab him."

Miss Gusta grab him? The best looking gentleman caller Aunt Matilda had ever had? Suddenly I knew exactly whom Aunt Creola was talking about. Yes, I knew as well as I knew my name that it could only be Mr. Ed Alston who had come and gone while I was away.

"For goodness sakes, Aunt Creola!" said Aunt Matilda. "That was a million years ago. Why on earth should you remember it now?"

"Because he ain't got past rememberin' it. That's why. While I was servin' the 'freshments ev'ry time I look at him, he was peepin' over to where you was settin' at."

"Probably thinking how old and fat and ugly I've come to be."

"Well you is more fleshy than what you was, but you's still a fine lookin' lady—which he could see as well as me," insisted Aunt Creola.

"We'll say no more about it," Aunt Matilda told her firmly. "It's just too ridiculous to even think about."

"Except for one more thing," Aunt Creola persisted. "I'll bet my new set of false teeth that if Miss Gusta—if she was to pass—he'd be right back out here, settin' on the porch just like he was today."

Aunt Creola had said it—and out loud, too, the same thing I had often thought about and which Aunt Mary Lou could never bring herself to put into words—but to this remark, Aunt Matilda did not even deign to reply. Instead, she came out onto the front porch, where Aunt Mary Lou was reading The Episcopal Herald and I had perched on the porch steps.

For a moment Aunt Matilda stood viewing the streamers of coral and gold that stitched together the sagging sunset clouds beyond the trees. When she spoke at last, however, she asked a question that was so different from the subject at hand and so astonishing that I could hardly believe I had heard what she said.

"Child," she asked, "what would you think if your Aunt Mary Lou and I decided to buy a house in town?"

A house in town! That was the last thing I could imagine the sisters doing!

"But if you did that," I cried, "why, I couldn't come out here to visit you!" And my heart seemed to be about to break at the very thought. "I couldn't bear not coming!"

"Of course, you could come to visit. We'd only stay in town for the colder winter months. We'd be right here in the early fall, the late spring, and of course, in the summer."

Aunt Mary Lou stopped reading to explain. "The doctor thinks it's a very good idea, now that we're getting older. Besides, he has a difficult time driving his gig out here when the roads are deep in mud."

"We'd only want a little house," continued Aunt Matilda. "Not far from the center of town and close to the hospital—in case either of us should get sick."

"And close to the church," added Aunt Mary Lou. "So we could attend service every Sunday."

"We'll start looking for a suitable place right away," said Aunt Matilda in the firm decisive way in which she always spoke after she had put her mind on a problem and had already decided what to do.

But a house in town! I knew I could never get used to it and would never like it, no matter what sort of a house it turned out to be, but in this I was mistaken.

## Chapter Eight

*Bessie Cow — Pete and Repeat — Village Scandals — The Fancy Lady — Aunt Matilda's Portrait — Edward*

### 8.

The new home in town turned out to be just what the sisters wanted.

A little white house, only one story in height with a porch across the front where the sisters could sit when the weather permitted, it had a small but pretty front yard where crocus blooms and violets peeped up through the grass in spring. It also had a large grassy back lot that the ladies said would make a perfect grazing place for Bessie, the docile brown and white cow that, to the astonishment and strong disapproval of my parents, they planned to bring to town.

That Bessie was to accompany them was due to the fact that neither lady "trusted city milk" and Aunt Matilda had no intention of doing without "pure fresh cream" for her morning coffee and "pure, fresh whipped cream" for the Chocolate Blanc Mange, Charlotte Russe, Floating Island, and other old-fashioned desserts that she enjoyed.

My parents tried to dissuade them from bringing Bessie, but both ladies were adamant about fetching her, and, as soon as the house was made comfortable, Bessie appeared. With her came black and genial May Ella, who tended her. The two gained instant popularity with the children in our neighborhood, since there were no cows dwelling there and no cow handmaidens either. A small white painted house was built for Bessie at the far end of the grassy back lot and with it Bessie, May Ella, Estelle, Aunt Mary Lou, and Aunt Matilda were quite pleased.

"Not trusting city milk," the two ladies also "did not trust city water," so at first they were all for having an artesian well like the one at Bellevue dug close to the back door. In the end, however, this idea was put to rest by Mr. Pinkney Hilderbrand, the chief tenant at Bellevue, whom we children called Mr. Pink. He came riding into town at regular intervals in a large farm wagon behind a pair of twin mules named Pete and Repeat, bringing with him a number of gallon size glass jugs full of water from the well at Bellevue.

Something else that Mr. Pink brought to town was a hat tub; for Aunt Mary Lou said she saw "no reason to break with tradition" at their late time of life. She also said she thought it would be dangerous for a lady of Aunt Matilda's plumpness to attempt to climb up into or down out of the bathtubs in the new home. However, at this, Aunt Matilda, who had ideas of her own, was inclined to balk.

"You have never had the proper regard for the styles, Mary Lou," she argued. "And now that we are in town, we might as well try out the modern way."

"That's entirely beside the point, Matilda. Suppose you should slip and fall," Aunt Mary Lou said, remembering that a younger sister, who was also inclined toward corpulency, had once fallen while engaged in such activity and had cracked several ribs. "Besides, I really think this tub can be used for a more advantageous purpose."

"Like what, for instance?" demanded Aunt Matilda.

"Well, frankly, I've been worried about those lovely apples that were brought in from the orchard at home. They'll surely rot if they're not laid out in some nice, cool place."

This gave Aunt Matilda pause. She could not deny that she enjoyed a fine, homegrown apple—a Magnum Bonum or a Golden Delicious or a Limbertwig—and she was especially fond of apple pie; so at first it was the apples that occupied the big white tub in their bathroom while she and Aunt Mary Lou continued to use the hat tub, just as they had all during the past years.

The house in town had hot air heating that was furnished by a coal furnace in the cellar directly under a large, round black iron grill in the floor of the front hall, and this invention, that was new at the time and supposed to heat the whole house, gave the sisters some uneasy thoughts. At the old home in the country each room had its own fireplace, which they thought was much safer than having a fire in the bowels of the earth directly beneath them where, for all one knew, an explosion could take place and send both of them shooting through the roof at any moment.

It took several conversations with my father to convince them that the heat should be turned on at all times during the cold months, but they kept it turned low and sent one of the servants to the cellar at intervals, to see if anything happened to be amiss. They also kept fires burning in the parlor and in their bedroom, in case the new-fangled furnace blew up or broke down.

They were disappointed that Aunt Creola, who had been the cook in the country for many years, said she was just too old to go with them and "take on city ways." She sent in her place her niece, Fanny, who was also an excellent cook.

Sam, of the opossum catching fame, agreed to come to town

whenever needed to mow grass, clip shrubbery and attend to other chores, and since the ladies brought in no horse and vehicle, Uncle Ike promised to arrange for the horse and the Low Buggy to be driven to town whenever the sisters wished. The surrey had gone out of style with the coming of the automobile and the buggy was becoming passé, too, but Aunt Matilda agreed with this idea because it at least offered a way of getting about.

At length, with all these pressing matters arranged satisfactorily, the sisters settled down in their new quarters. They began to take an interest in their environs, and being strong Episcopalians, they soon received a shock on learning of a much talked about scandal in which the rector of the Episcopal Church was involved.

How this particular gentleman had ever become the shepherd of our small parish was never exactly clear. To begin with, he was an Englishman with a British accent that did not fall easily upon Southern ears, and, to cap it all, he was "high" church whereas we were "low."

He was tall, thin, long-nosed and stern looking on the order of Basil Rathbone, the movie actor, and after church he removed only his white surplice and went about town on Sundays and weekdays, too if he desired to do so, with his long black cassock flapping at his heels. A large silver cross that hung on a silver chain upon his chest flashed in the sun, and on his head there sat a three cornered biretta with a pom-pom atop it, the likes of which many of the villagers had never clapped eyes upon before.

The pride of the Presbyterians in their superior spirituality was well-known in town, and a tale had even been circulated about an old Presbyterian Session book that was found in the rubble of the first Courthouse when it was torn down in order for a new one to be built.

In the first Courthouse the various church congregations had taken turns having services before the churches were built and the session book had somehow slipped into a crack and had not been found. Then it unexpectedly came to light, and the questions put to the elders at certain meetings were discovered.

According to the story—which may well have been true—one question went something like this: "What shall we do about these ungodly Episcopalians who have moved into our midst?" And the answer, also duly recorded, was, "Treat them kindly but do not imitate their wicked ways."

It may have been partly due to this that the piety of the Episcopalians had been put into question, but the shenanigans of its minister caused it to fall even deeper when, without warning, on a Sunday morning he had an incense pot swung, filling the little church with the hitherto unknown—and, to some members, diabolical—aroma. Not long after this, a tale went out that the gentleman was indulging in an affair with a beautiful married lady of his flock. Of course, tongues started wagging, and they began to wag even faster when an astonishing event involving the two took place.

The lady in question had a rather ample bosom and was in the habit of wearing dresses cut somewhat low and loosely arranged at the neck, and it was just such a dress that she was wearing when the minister and she happened to meet one spring morning on the Courthouse Square. At sight of her, he exclaimed with such delight that his false teeth—of which no one had been aware until that moment—sprang out of his mouth, and while passersby paused, startled by this unexpected turn of events, disappeared down the low cut neck of the lady's dress.

We learned later that it was not a full set of teeth but a more modest arrangement with only five or six teeth attached to a gold wire frame. Regardless of the number of teeth, the Episcopal Vestry, stunned by such goings-on, went into action and it was not long before the erring gentleman was sent on his way.

In time he was replaced by another gentleman of the cloth who conducted himself in a more traditional manner. He wore his robes only during church services. The incense pot disappeared and we became "low church" again—until another catastrophe occurred, which was even worse.

The new rector had a wife and a small child. The wife died and the ladies of the church, touched by his youth and single state, immediately took him in tow. Collectively, they saw to it that the rectory was run in a proper fashion and they kept the path hot to his door, fetching delicacies for his table—going in person on these occasions to see for themselves how things were coming along.

When a respectable period of mourning had passed, they made it their object to find for him a wife who would not only be a suitable mate, but could also become an ornament to the parish. Therefore their joy knew no bounds when such a lady was found and the rector took to the bait.

During the courtship and marriage that followed, the ladies lived in a rosy haze, and when a child was born their happiness reached its peak. In fact they continued in this blissful state for a year or more, during which they were continuing to congratulate themselves upon the success of their endeavors, when a tale began to circulate that was worse than any lady could possibly have dreamed—a tale with a woman in it.

When Aunt Matilda heard the news, she sat bolt upright in her chair beside the parlor fire in the new little white house in town. She was so shocked that she even forgot that I was in the room. In fact, she seemed to be frozen in place, not blinking an eye as the overwhelming and scandalous information was poured into her always receptive ear by the elderly lady caller who had hot-footed it to her door as swiftly as her rheumatism would allow after she herself had heard the story.

After Aunt Matilda had gotten herself more in hand, she asked, "Is it anyone we know?"

The lady caller, who still had not fully recovered her equilibrium, was hardly able to reply, but she managed to gasp, "No! No! Heavens, no!"

"Then who is she?" Aunt Matilda demanded.

"It's no one you know, Matilda."

"I know almost everybody in town, so perhaps—"

"But not this one!" cried the lady caller as she got more control of herself. "She's—she's a—a fancy lady!"

A fancy lady? I was listening closely but this was a new one to me, and it must have been to Aunt Matilda, too, because she paused as she turned the information over in her mind.

"I never heard it called that before. Are you sure you heard correctly?"

"I'm sure. Perfectly sure! And she's said to be the—I mean—the main one in town! I wonder how on earth she and the rector could have met!" The lady caller gave a little shiver at the thought of it.

"That's neither here nor there, Hortense. So get yourself together. I've known about that woman for some time."

"But how could you? I mean—it's impossible, Matilda! Who could have told you?"

At once I thought about Estelle, May Ella and Fanny. The black people had what we called a "grapevine telegraph" that ran from one end of town to the other. It was said they knew about everything that went on before the white people did and I felt certain they told Aunt Matilda news they would never so much as hint to the pious Aunt Mary Lou.

"Oh, it's just too dreadful!" The lady caller mourned, "What on earth can be done?"

"He ought to be tarred and feathered and ridden out of town on a rail!" Aunt Matilda stated flatly. "The same goes for her. After all—she's nothing but a common prostitute, so—"

"Matilda! That word! The child is listening!"

For the first time Aunt Matilda's eye fell upon me. She quickly ordered me to go to the kitchen and tell Fanny to bring in some tea and refreshments. Consequently, I did not hear the following details of the rector's story, but I caught the lady caller's worried statement as I left the room.

"I don't think we'd better tell Mary Lou," she said. "The shock might affect her heart."

Of course, Aunt Mary Lou came to know the story, as did the whole town; so the Episcopal Vestry took the matter in hand. My father was Senior Warden at the time and the vestry quickly assembled. They called the young minister to task, at which time he demanded to know why the Episcopalians could not "whitewash their preacher as other churches in town were doing."

At this, the vestry was stunned. It entered into an investigation during which it discovered that the gentleman knew whereof he spoke. After this, it was not long before we became aware that a disturbance of sorts was taking place in the Baptist Church, and the Baptist preacher came afoul of the same accusation that had fallen upon the Episcopal rector. We did not hear a great deal about it, for the details were kept rather quiet, but the Baptist preacher left town and not long after this a young and pretty married lady who sang in his choir also disappeared.

As if all this was not enough to paralyze the entire village, a third story began to ripple through the community that said the Methodist preacher and the hotel keeper's wife were in the same boat, so to speak. At any rate, it was not long before he and his wife moved away, to operate another hostelry in another town.

As for the Episcopal rector, he was defrocked and he, too, left town, but he did not go alone. With him went the fancy lady.

Naturally, it took some time for the sisters, and for the whole town, to get over these soul-shaking events, but Aunt Mary Lou and Aunt Matilda were finally able to put their minds to an important matter from which they had been diverted by the scandalous behavior of the three village "divines," and this was to have a portrait painted of Aunt Matilda.

# Chapter Eight

How this important matter had been neglected during the years they could not understand, for both ladies realized it was unthinkable for future generations to be deprived of knowing what a fine looking lady Aunt Matilda was. It did not appear to occur to them that she was no longer the slender, ravishing creature she once had been; so they summoned a portrait painter and Aunt Matilda sat for her portrait, dressed in her best.

When the artist finished, however, neither lady was satisfied. Aunt Mary Lou objected particularly to "the grim look about the mouth." She said there should be a slight curve to the lips, a half smile that gave a hint of the good humor and ready wit that Aunt Matilda possessed.

The artist was called back several times but was never able to accomplish this, so after a while the ladies dismissed him and had the portrait hung in the little home in town over the big flat topped piano that had ivory keys and lamp holders covered with crimson velvet at each end of the keyboard.

We wondered why the sisters had brought the huge, old-fashioned piano to town, where the rooms were so much smaller than those in the country, especially since they never played upon it, but we realized they must have a certain indefinable nostalgic attachment to it that we did not understand. They always referred to it as "Mother's piano" and from time to time they reminisced about the days of long ago when their mother gathered her children about her and they all sang together while she played, or danced to the music in the big high-ceilinged parlor at Bellevue. Thus, perhaps in bringing the piano, they were also bringing with it happy childhood memories in which they took pleasure in retrospect.

A few days after the portrait was hung, I went to pay a call on my aunts and was astonished to find the tall, black clad Aunt Mary Lou standing on the flat top of the piano. In one hand she held an artist's palette with daubs of paint upon it and in the other a paint brush, with which she was applying paint to the portrait.

When I inquired what she was doing, she replied, "My child, I'm painting a smile on your Aunt Matilda's face."

Although Aunt Mary Lou was skilled at painting landscapes, portraiture was not her forte, so the most that could be said for her efforts was that the corners of Aunt Matilda's mouth turned up, whereas formerly they had turned down. Not wanting to hurt her feelings, we kept silent, but in time she, too, realized she had not exactly hit the nail on the head, as the saying goes; so she mounted the piano again, palette and brush in hand, and followed a new idea—which was to mostly conceal the mouth by painting greyish-brown shadows over the lower part of the face.

When my mother inquired of my father, who was the first member of the family to view the finished product, what he thought of the newly applied shadows, he replied, "It looks as though Sister Matilda has grown a beard."

Aunt Mary Lou, still not satisfied with her handiwork, decided to make one more try. She mounted the piano again and was able to erase some of the beard that hid a good part of the mouth and chin, but after that, the portrait bore so little likeness to Aunt Matilda as to be almost unrecognizable. Still, I must confess that when I went calling on the aunts, it was a relief not to have a lady with a beard, who looked as though she had just escaped from the circus, always watching us from the parlor wall.

Although my aunts did not agree with each other on every subject, they lived together pleasantly and without any major altercation. In spite of their being so unalike, it was easy to see that they were devoted to each other, and in thinking of this, I am reminded of the only time I knew them to come close to what could have turned into a real quarrel.

As Aunt Matilda grew older and the rheumatism in her knees grew worse, she could not get about as she had in the past. Since she always wanted to keep up with what was going on in the community, she often sent Aunt Mary Lou, "the fleet of foot," foraging for news, and I remember one afternoon after school when I stopped by to see them and found that Aunt Mary Lou was preparing to leave on such an errand.

"Just stop by to see Minerva, Laura and Ella," Aunt Matilda directed her, mentioning three elderly sisters who lived not far away. "I hear they've all been sick. Inquire how they are and be sure to get the news."

"All right, Matilda," Aunt Mary Lou answered mechanically.

"And you might stop to see Lizzie and Maggie McDowell," she added, referring to two elderly lady cousins. "They usually know what's going on. But don't start talking genealogy. You won't get back until after dark if you do."

"I'll do just as you say, Matilda," answered Aunt Mary Lou.

"And you might go by Kibler's Drug Store—it's right on your way—and get some peppermint drops."

## Chapter Eight

"That's just what I'll do, Matilda. I'll be ready to go in a minute, when I get my Talma."

The Talma was a long black voluminous cape that covered Aunt Mary Lou from her chin to her toes. It was named after General Talma, an officer on the Duke of Wellington's staff, and it was just such a garment that he was wearing when he met Napoleon at Waterloo. Once it had been quite fashionable, but it had long since gone out of style, so even the sight of it irritated Aunt Matilda every time she looked upon it; and she had urged Aunt Mary Lou to buy a new and more stylish garment for several years, but without result.

Since it afforded Aunt Mary Lou protection from the weather, was modest, comfortable and durable (which was all she asked of a garment), she had continued to wear it in spite of her sister's protests. As she put on the Talma—while Aunt Matilda watched with her usual disapproval—she took down her hat from the closet shelf and placed it upon her head but at this, Aunt Matilda let out a yell that stopped Aunt Mary Lou in her tracks.

"What is it, Matilda?" she cried, very much frightened and certain her sister was having an attack of some sort.

Aunt Matilda rolled her eyes to the heavens like the people in the pictures of the martyrs of old who were in agony while being burned at the stake. "Just look at her, child!" she exclaimed, waving a hand toward Aunt Mary Lou, who was still galvanized with fright and waiting to see how things would turn out. "You are seeing a sight you have never beheld before and one that you will never see again! There stands before you the only woman in Christendom who puts her hat on backwards—without a single glance in the mirror— and is willing to go forth and face the world in that condition!"

"Oh, is that all?" Aunt Mary Lou slumped with relief. "I thought you might be dying—or, at least, in terrible pain."

"I am in pain!" Aunt Matilda shouted. "But I'm not so far gone that I'll let you go out and face the public with your hat on backwards! If you think I'm going to let you disgrace this family in such a way, you're badly mistaken!"

Aunt Mary Lou, who still looked weak after the shock she had just experienced, took hold of her hat brim with two fingers and gingerly gave it a twitch to one side.

"Is it straight now?"

"No, it is not!"

Aunt Mary Lou gave the hat brim another twitch. "What about now?"

For Aunt Matilda this was just too much to be borne. Wincing at the pain in her knees, she heaved herself from her chair and jerked the hat straight on Aunt Mary Lou's head.

"You look a perfect fright!" she declared. "And if I don't do something about it, who will?"

She grabbed the front of the Talma, marched Aunt Mary Lou to the bureau, seized her big pink marabou powder puff, dipped it into her box of white rice face powder, the only kind available in that day, and slapped the puff so vigorously over Aunt Mary Lou's face that a cloud of white powder enveloped both of them.

At the first blow of the puff, Aunt Mary Lou instinctively shut her eyes and screwed up her face; so when she opened her eyes to peep out at Aunt Matilda, to see what she might be up to next, there was a network of lines and wrinkles all over her face into which the powder had not penetrated.

This was not at all the effect Aunt Matilda had sought or expected to see, so, enraged at the very sight, she set to work scrubbing off the excess powder. She sent Estelle for a damp towel to finish the job and then for a dry one and also a whiskbroom and clothes brush. She even called Fannie in from the kitchen to help. Then, after both ladies had been dusted off, Aunt Matilda was so exhausted and felt so undone that, as a restorative measure, she uncorked her bottle of violet cologne, sprinkled some upon herself and then some upon Aunt Mary Lou, who, although she never used cologne or cosmetics of any sort, submitted meekly to her sister's ministrations.

"My child," Aunt Matilda said as she sank into her chair and Aunt Mary Lou went upon her way, "Someday I'm going to have a high seat in heaven for living with that woman here on earth!"

As time went by and the ladies grew older, they found it easier to spend more time in town and less time in the country, but there came a year when, after a cold and rainy winter and early spring, a summer followed with a wealth of sunshine and flowers. Encouraged by such golden days, they decided to go home earlier than usual, to spend a longer than usual visit at the old home on the hill, and they invited me to go along.

I was delighted to do so and had no premonition that the visit might be the only one of such length they would ever again spend at the old home. When we arrived at Bellevue, Aunt Matilda, seeming to gain extra energy, went to work as quickly as possible in her beloved flower garden and Aunt Mary Lou and I rambled about the woods and meadows, not tramping as far as we had in the past but enjoying the outings greatly.

We were disappointed to find that the old road, down which we had ridden so often in the High Buggy to cross the river, was so overgrown with weeds and brambles that the buggy tracks of former years could hardly be seen.

Later I was to learn that the river fording place was closed. It saddened me to think that no other little girl would ever know that there had once been a fording place there with a sandbar in the middle where the water was so shallow and clear that it looked golden as it rippled over the yellow sand beneath it and the minnows darted like quick silver about one's feet. It seemed to be impossible that the old fording place would never be used again. Still, I was comforted in knowing that Aunt Mary Lou and I would remember it. It would be our secret, never to be forgotten—a secret that would belong only to us, no matter how long we lived.

On one afternoon during that visit at the old home, Aunt Matilda requested that Aunt Mary Lou and I carry a cake that Aunt Creola had just baked to "the Perkins girls"—three elderly ladies who were their close friends and lived about six miles up the valley. We went in the Low Buggy and had such a pleasant time that we returned home later than planned. As we came close enough to get a good look at the house on the hill, Aunt Mary Lou suddenly leaned forward and adjusted her spectacles.

"Look, child," she said. "Isn't that a gasoline machine leaving the house and coming down the avenue?"

I looked and she was right. It was a long black automobile that was called a "touring machine" in that day, and was open on each side. There was a black driver at the wheel, and, to my surprise and delight, seated alone in the rear was Mr. Ed Alston. I knew that Cousin Augusta had died the preceding year and I had not seen him during that time. However, I knew I had to allow for a proper period of mourning and I still had not given up on my hopes for him and Aunt Matilda.

At the sight, a sudden thrill went over me and as the automobile turned into the public road just ahead of us, I took a good look at him and saw that he was still a fine looking gentleman in spite of his age. He had taken off his hat because of the heat of the day, and I could see his crest of silver hair and his still handsome profile, which the ladies admired so greatly.

"Bless my soul!" exclaimed Aunt Mary Lou. "It's Edward

Alston!"

We found Aunt Matilda sitting on the front porch, wearing one of her most becoming dresses. She had on her diamond earrings, too.

"I thought I saw Edward Alston coming down the avenue in a gasoline machine," Aunt Mary Lou told her.

"That is correct," answered Aunt Matilda.

There was a silence while Aunt Mary Lou pondered the situation. "He addressed you, of course," she said.

Aunt Matilda smiled. "Ask me no questions and I'll tell you no lies."

There was another silence, longer than the first. Then Aunt Mary Lou ventured, "I hope I had no part in it."

"What do you mean by that, Mary Lou?"

"I mean—well, I mean that you should not feel any guilt about leaving me. I could get along very well—that is, in town. Of course, you'd want to take Estelle with you, but Fanny is an excellent cook and I could put May Ella in the little back bedroom, where she would be close by if I needed her."

"Oh, Mary Lou—always so self-sacrificing and self-denying!" replied Aunt Matilda.

"But I would never for an instant stand in the way of your happiness, Matilda."

"Happiness! With that old goat?"

Old goat! I was astounded. I could not believe what I was hearing. The Prince Charming of Aunt Matilda's youth, whom, I felt, she still worshipped, just as she had during all the long years and who still worshipped her.

Aunt Matilda looked out across the valley at the distant mountains that had a gauzy pink haze upon their peaks now that sunset was coming on. "Frankly, Mary Lou, I don't think Edward was ever as smart as I used to think he was. And you know, I never could stand a man who had less sense than I did. Why, this afternoon he told me that the first thing he did after the war was to sell Riverside."

"But the planters had no choice. The Yankees put the taxes so high they couldn't pay them and they had to sell!" countered Aunt Mary Lou.

"Well, all the same, if Edward had been married to me I wouldn't have allowed it!" Aunt Matilda retorted with emphasis. "Riverside was one of the best cotton growing plantations in the state. Somehow I'd have hung onto it and kept on raising cotton to beat the band. Even if the Yankees did lick us, he should have had more

## Chapter Eight

sense than that."

Aunt Mary Lou set her jaw and into her eyes came a steely, unyielding glint that made me aware that under her compassionate and yielding gentleness, there was a vein of iron that could not be broken or chipped away.

"We were not licked, Matilda. We were overrun by a more numerous and better equipped foe, but the Lord will enable us to rise again. In His good time, the country will know of what metal we Southerners are made. Until then, we must try to forgive our enemies and serve the Lord in every way."

"Well, isn't that what we've been trying to do?" demanded Aunt Matilda.

"Yes, and that's why we've gotten on as well as we have."

"But not always," Aunt Matilda corrected her. "Now that you've brought up the subject, I might as well confess that there have been times when I didn't feel very forgiving towards our enemies, or even towards you—times when I really felt like wringing your neck—when something important had to be done and you just kept standing there saying, 'The Lord will provide.'"

"Well, He did, Matilda. He has." Aunt Mary Lou paused and sighed. "I've always regretted that I haven't helped you more in running the place, but you have a head that's so much better for business than mine that—"

"Thank goodness you didn't try to help! It would have driven me stark, raving crazy to have you always butting in. As it was, you've done your way, and I've done mine. You've lived your life and I've lived mine—so we rarely got in each other's way."

As I listened to Aunt Matilda, I suddenly realized that, unknowingly, she had given the correct reply to the question that no one else had ever been able to answer—the question as to how the sisters, who were so different, had managed to live together such peaceful and contented—but altogether different—lives all through the long years under the same roof in the same old house on the hill.

Our visit to Bellevue had been so pleasant that, as we drove back to town that summer afternoon, I was in a happy mood, in spite of what Aunt Matilda had said about Mr. Ed Alston; so I was in no way prepared for the shocking event that the sisters told me would shortly come to pass.

*The Last House Party — A Lesson in Love and Generosity  
— The Angel of Death — Voices in the Night*

### 9.

As we drove back to Morganton in the Low Buggy on that summer afternoon, my aunts told me that the old home was going to be dismantled—all of its rooms stripped bare and the furnishings divided. The land, the house and all the household furnishings had been left by their mother in equal shares among her children, all of whom would be coming soon to a last family house party, to attend to the dividing.

"Then this was our last visit!" I exclaimed in distress.

"All things on earth come to an end, child," said Aunt Mary Lou. "So it's better this way. We've known for some time it would have to come to this. Your Aunt Matilda and I are growing older every day."

"The house just can't be left standing on the hill, packed with furniture and other things, with no one to take care of it," added Aunt Matilda.

"'Where moths corrupt and thieves break through and steal,'" said Aunt Mary Lou, putting an apt Bible quotation into the conversation, as she often did.

I dreaded the last family house party, but it turned out to be far more pleasant than I had expected. Some of my aunts and uncles stayed at the old home and some at our house in town. All of them appeared to be bent on making the occasion as happy as possible, even though I knew their hearts were sad, as was mine.

I was impressed anew by their affection and consideration for each other; and in remembering that day, I realize that it was then that I learned a lesson in kindness, unselfishness, generosity and love that I have never forgotten and for which I will always be grateful. Each brother and sister seemed to want to put their brothers and sisters before themselves and to see to it that no one felt slighted or denied and that each received equal treatment and obtained what each one wanted most.

The only part of the day that was sad and difficult came when it was ending, when the front door was locked with the huge, old-fashioned brass key and we drove away, leaving behind us the beloved old home standing bereft and alone upon the hill.

It was hard to even look back—to see its windows staring after

## Chapter Nine

us, watching as we rode away. But perhaps there were ghosts looking out from behind those empty, staring windows—the ghosts of those who had long ago gone their way, but now came crowding back into the quiet, empty rooms to look out at the surrounding meadows and fields, the bottom lands and the faraway mountains—just as we ourselves had done so many times—and it was they who would take care of the old home while it waited for us to return.

About a year after the house was emptied and closed, Aunt Creola, the cook at Bellevue, passed away. Then came the death of Aunt Betsy, the wife of Uncle Ike, and the old man was miserable without her. His rheumatism had been growing worse and he wept when he confided to Aunt Mary Lou and Aunt Matilda that his hands were sometimes so twisted with pain that he could no longer handle the horses and drive the surrey. The sisters, seeing his misery, shed a few tears, too, and they were deeply touched by his sadness and pain.

When he said he had decided to move to town to live with his daughter, Della, and her family, the ladies thought well of it. We were glad that Della's home was not far from ours. It was just down the hill in back of us, where Aunt Claudia's Emma, who had passed away, once lived—the Emma whom Jim had so often ridden home in the wheelbarrow when Aunt Claudia said she was "indisposed."

At first, after Uncle Ike moved to town, it gave me a start to see him come limping up onto our street because he seemed to be so out of place. However, I always knew he was on his way to "pay respects to my ladies," and the more I thought about it, the more natural it seemed to be. After all, he belonged to the sisters and they belonged to him. He was theirs and they were his. The long association between them through the years had woven a bond that nothing but death could break. I knew this and the three of them knew it, too.

One winter morning during the Christmas holidays when I did not have to be in school, I sat with my aunts and the faithful Estelle about their parlor fire. Fanny, who was the cook in town, announced that Uncle Ike had arrived; I remember the quaint old-fashioned way he "pulled his foot and made his bow" as he took off his hat.

"I pays you ladies my respects," he said with old-time courtesy. Then in spite of his rheumatism, he also bobbed in a bow to me. "And respects to you, too, lil Missy."

"Come in, Uncle Ike, and get warm by the fire," the sisters chorused, at which Estelle placed a chair for him to sit with us at the hearth, where he stretched out his gnarled old hands to the blaze.

"It's too cold for you to go rambling around in this sort of weather," Aunt Matilda said. "You should take better care of yourself."

"It the truth, but somehow I had a cravin' to take a peep-in at you ladies. How has you been farin'?"

"About the same," Aunt Mary Lou told him. Noticing that he still shook with cold, she added, "Estelle will get you a nice hot cup of coffee. That ought to warm you."

"Yes, ma'am. Thanky, ma'am. The ole man would be pleasured with a nice cup of coffee. Seems like the cold done bit to the bone."

When Estelle brought the coffee, his shaky old hands rattled the cup against the saucer, but he drank with relish and as he relaxed he began to talk about the old home on the hill.

"How the old home place comin' along with us gone away?" he asked.

"About the same, I hope," said Aunt Matilda.

"I hear tell as how Ole Pal, he up and died," he replied.

"So we heard," Aunt Mary Lou told him.

"Ole Pal, he the strongest mule on the place for haulin'—never slowed up or got tired. But Lucy, now—she the best at the plow." He sipped his coffee and waited, his thoughts drifting back in time. "My pa, he started me to plowin' with Lucy when I wasn't no higher than a hoppergrass." He waited and pondered a moment. "I misses Lucy. I shorely does." His look brightened and he added, "Then come the day when yo' pa say I was ole enough and smart enough to set up in front on the high box of the carriage with Amos—he the coachman then—and learn to handle the horses." His rheumy old eyes glistened with reflections from the flames as he gazed into the fire, remembering. "Then come the time the rheumatiz hit Amos so bad he couldn't climb up onto the box of the carriage, so the very next Sunday I driv the family to church. Lawsee, me! I thought I was some punkin' then." He laughed and the sisters laughed with him. "That was when yo' pa had that pair of matched blacks—true bloods and spirituous—hard to handle. They was both high steppers, but I saw to it they got to know me pretty quick—my voice and my hands on the reins. Didn't have no trouble after that."

"Pa said you were the best coachman he ever had," Aunt Mary Lou told him.

"Did?" A pleased smile made the furrows deepen and change in

## Chapter Nine

his kind old black face. "Many's the times I'se driv you young misses to parties and frolics and such." He chuckled, making the sisters smile as they, too, remembered. "That young gentman what come all the way down from Baltimo' to 'dress you, Miss Mary Lou—you didn't waste no time in sendin' him back. And, Miss Matilda, you had a passel of gentmen callers—but Mr. Ed Alston—all the folks say he the best. He 'dressed you, too—but you turned round and handed him over to Miss Gusta." He paused and pondered again.

The pain in his old limbs would not let him rest, so he twisted and turned in his chair while we listened to the crackling of the fire and to the wind as it drove against the window panes.

"Seems like I hear tell, Mister Ed Alston, he done died," he ventured after a moment.

"No. That was his wife," Aunt Matilda told him.

"Was? Well, that's too bad." He shook his head and waited. Then his thoughts turned back to the old home place again. "I shorely would like to go back to the old home, drive all over and see what's gwine on."

"I hope you can," said Aunt Mary Lou. "When the warm weather comes you ought to feel better."

"Mebbe so. Mebbe so." He picked up his walking stick from where it lay beside his chair on the floor. Then he rose unsteadily to his feet.

"Just a minute," Aunt Matilda said. "Fanny baked a nice cake yesterday and I want you to take some for yourself and Della's family—and some gingerbread men for the children. Estelle will get them for you."

"That'll be nice, mighty nice. Just put 'em in one of them paper pokes. That'll make 'em easy to carry."

While he waited, standing there in the firelight, stooped and unsteady and leaning on his cane, I thought how old and tired he looked and wondered if that visit might be his last to "pay respects to his ladies."

Then I was surprised to hear him say, "I'll be back soon if the Angel of Death don't come first, knockin' on my door."

At that moment I would have found it impossible to believe that he would outlive both sisters, lingering on to be over a hundred years old—and that for many more years, I would see Fanny or May Ella or Estelle carrying Thanksgiving and Christmas baskets down the hill to Della's house. Big white damask napkins would cover the baskets and hide their contents but underneath there would be a roast turkey, rice and gravy, sweet potato pudding, cranberry sauce, and other foods the sisters knew he enjoyed. Nor did I guess that there would be nights when the old man thought the Angel of Death was knocking at his door and had come to carry him off—before that final Sunday morning when the Angel really came and took him away.

Deep in the night, wakened in my bed, at times I would hear a timid but urgent knocking on our back door and hear one of Della's little boys say in a childish voice, "Please, suh—Grandpa, he say the Angel of Death done come, and he say—please, suh—he craves to hear you read the Bible one mo' time and say a prayer befo' the Angel fetch him off."

While the little black boy faded into the shadows as silently as he had come, my father would fling on some clothes to go to Della's house to read the Bible and pray with Uncle Ike, and I remember especially one moonlit night when I went to stand at my bedroom window to see a tall man striding hurriedly down our side lawn on his way to Della's, his Bible under his arm and his shadow following him along the moon whitened grass.

One night he stayed at Della's until morning, but when he left there the Angel had flown away without taking Uncle Ike, which had happened many times before.

It was not only Della's little boys who came quietly and without warning to our house at night, however. There were others who came but never knocked. When I was quite young, I was frightened one night when I heard footsteps on the driveway beneath my window and saw a tall black man in the bright moonlight heading toward our stable.

When I hurried to tell my father, he only said, "Oh, it's just one of the boys from the old homeplace. He feels this is his home, too, and knows he's welcome. He probably had a big day in town and got left by the wagon. He'll get a good night's sleep in the hay in the stable loft and be gone by morning."

After that I was never frightened when I heard footsteps and voices whispering in the dark, for sometimes they came in small groups, and it was usually on Saturday nights—for the black men liked to spend Saturdays in town. Sometimes several of the women came in on Saturdays, too, bringing with them infants and children too small to leave at home, and on these occasions a little group always turned up at our house for midday dinner. Anticipating this, Alice had Jim up early on Saturday mornings, wringing the necks of chickens that she was going to fry. She also cooked extra vegetables from the garden and made additional pans of cornbread, so there would be enough for all.

The black women, knowing they were welcome and expected since they came from Bellevue, shyly but proudly carried their babies and herded their children who were a little older and could walk, around the side of the house, and we made a point of welcoming them, while Alice was in her glory, playing hostess.

If the weather was pleasant, she placed the children on the steps of our wide back porch which was on the other side of the house from the grazing lot, where they perched politely and quietly, like birds along the top of a fence, waiting with anticipation for whatever food Alice would give them—especially the desserts, which were usually some sort of pie.

We knew that after dinner they would go by "to pay respects to Miss Matilda and Miss Mary Lou," and that Aunt Matilda always had a cookie for each of the children while Aunt Mary Lou dispensed to the older ones religious cards with illustrated Bible verses upon them. Then, after this, they would rejoin the Saturday crowd down on Main Street near the Courthouse before boarding the wagons to go back to the country.

Aunt Matilda died suddenly of a stroke when she was almost eighty-nine years old, her keen mind clear and alert to the end. She was buried beside her parents in the little graveyard of Grace Episcopal Church in Morganton, and Aunt Mary Lou was without her sister for the first time since she was less than two years old.

Her loneliness must have been acute after Aunt Matilda's death, but as usual, she never complained, although there were times when she spoke with a certain wistfulness of "Pa, Mother, and Matilda, who are on the other side." Then we felt that she was longing to join them.

She had never given up her habit of reading her Prayer Book and Bible and saying her prayers every morning. She also continued to be interested in national and international affairs and she became intrigued with the situation in China and Chiang Kai-shek, the Chinese leader about whom much was being printed in the newspapers at that time.

Although she was not so "fleet of foot" as she had been in the past, she never became stooped or slow of movement. Instead, she retained her slender, erect figure and her firm sure step. Still, we could see that she was growing slowly more frail and that a subtle change had come upon her that stemmed from Aunt Matilda's death.

Sometimes when the weather was good, she expressed the desire to "go home for a little while" —which meant an hour or so at the old house on the hill. At such times, she took with her the huge old-fashioned brass key to the front door, but she seldom used it. Perhaps she could not bear to enter the empty, silent, high ceilinged old rooms where only shadows and memories awaited her instead of the many loved ones who used to greet her long ago.

Sometimes she just strolled about the lawn, seeming to note each bush and flower and blade of grass. Usually, however, she sat quietly on the front porch, looking at the surrounding fields and meadows, the bottom lands and the distant mountains that seemed to hold the valley in their embrace while at the same time reaching forever upward to the continually changing sky. Then I wondered what memories came crowding back to her from the corners and recesses of her mind.

During the last year of her life, she looked so frail that her two younger sisters, Adelaide and Claudia, came to spend some time with her, feeling certain that death could not be far away. One night her breathing became so shallow and she lay so quietly that they sat up with her all night, fearing that she could not last until morning.

When dawn tinted the sky, however, she startled them by saying in a clear, firm voice, "I've been lying here thinking about the present situation in China. Can you tell me the latest news about Chiang Kai-shek?"

She died a few months later at the age of ninety-two, her mind, like Aunt Matilda's, alert and clear to the end. As one relative said, "She simply lay down and went to sleep as quietly as she had lived."

She was buried in the little graveyard of Grace Episcopal Church in Morganton beside her beloved Pa, Mother, and Matilda, and it was then, after she was no longer with us, that we were aware as never before that while she still breathed and lived, a saint had dwelt and walked amongst us.

## Chapter Ten

*Voices in the Wind*

*"What voices speak in the ever blowing winds—
from the forgotten days, the lost days—
if we but had the ears to hear them."*

### 10.

The Alder Spring from which the village took its first name has long since disappeared.

The people about whom I have written have gone their way, never to walk its streets again. Yet they linger with me still.

Beautiful Aunt Claudia works in her rose garden in the late summer afternoons.

The Witch Lady takes her daily walk, leaning on her gold-headed cane.

And Polly Malindy rides by in her wagon behind a big brown mule named Zeke.

In the valley an old home stands locked and silent on a hill.

Yet if one paused to listen, perhaps voices could be heard, caught forever in the river breeze that passes endlessly about its old brick walls:

The voices of children of different generations, calling in play across the sloping lawn—

Voices singing at twilight on the shadowy front porch—

The voices of "our men," the patriots, talking guardedly in the cave in the steep hillside above the creek, where they escaped from the enemy during the War of the Revolution.

Perhaps, even, the voice of a young mother named Sarah, who was soon to die for trying to save the life of a patriot, singing to her baby in that unforgotten house in the bottom lands.

For me, "The Gem in the Wilderness" lives on, its people and those of its environs, and I am grateful that I knew them when I could appreciate them most—when my heart was young in the morning of my life.

**THE END**

## Morganton 19th Nov 1816

Richard I. Church Dr
2 p Stirrups — 37½ — .75

David Tate Dr — .7½
½ doz of Iron Spoons — — .7½

Richard I. Church Dr
1 pr Strawning Webb — 2,75 — 2.75
3 yds Blue Homespun — 75 — 2.25

James Erwin Dr
1 Quire Paper — .32

Milton Ladd Dr
1 pr Worsted Hose — 1.12½

Dor. Jo A Tate Dr
2 p Stocking — 1.12½ — 2.25

Saml Roberts Dr
10" Sugar — 2.—
2¾" Coffee — 

George Sigman Dr
5" Coffee — 2.—

James Erwin Dr
1 Gro Small Buttons — 1.12